FOUNDATIONS *of* WRITING

Developing Research and Academic Writing Skills

FOUNDATIONS *of* WRITING

Developing Research and Academic Writing Skills

Carolyn M. Spencer • Beverly Arbon

National Textbook Company
a division of NTC/CONTEMPORARY PUBLISHING COMPANY
Lincolnwood, Illinois USA

Cover design by Nick Panos

1997 Printing

ISBN: 0-8442-9354-7

Published by National Textbook Company,
a division of NTC/Contemporary Publishing Company,
4255 West Touhy Avenue,
Lincolnwood (Chicago), Illinois 60646-1975 U.S.A.
©1996 by NTC/Contemporary Publishing Company
7 8 9 ML 0 9 8 7 6 5 4 3

Contents

Unit Five: *Defending a Position*   *155*

Unit Six: *Branching Out*   *187*

Unit Seven: *Applying Writing Skills to Essay Exams*   *215*

Appendix   *235*

Index   *244*

To the Student

You and your classmates are now in an academic writing class to learn about the types of writing that are required in American colleges and universities. Every student's writing experience has been different. Some have written mostly short letters or journal entries, while others have written in many different forms. Therefore, it is important at the beginning of this course to discuss the writing experience you and your classmates have had and what you expect from this class.

Consider these questions with your classmates:

1. How much writing have you done?
2. What kind of writing did you do? (stories, essays, reports)
3. What length were your writings? (number of paragraphs or pages)
4. What part of your writing experience did you enjoy?
5. What does the term *academic writing* mean to you?
6. What do you expect to learn from this class?

Here is a list of the types of writing that are generally required in colleges and universities. Look at this list together.

Put a *Y* for "yes" next to those you already know how to do.

Put a question mark (?) next to all those you need to know more about.

Put an *N* for "no" next to those you don't know.

- [ ] NOTES—you take notes from readings, interviews, or lectures
- [ ] LIBRARY RESEARCH—you use a library to find information for a research paper
- [ ] SUMMARIZE AN ARTICLE—you read an article and write the main ideas in a paragraph
- [ ] DESCRIPTION—you describe an event, a picture, or a place

☐ CAUSE AND EFFECT—you discuss the cause of something and how it affects something else

☐ COMPARISON AND CONTRAST—you discuss the similarities and differences of things or ideas

☐ PRO AND CON—you discuss two opposing sides of an issue

☐ ACADEMIC ARGUMENT—you look at both sides first, then take a position and defend it

☐ ANALYSIS—you carefully look at the parts of something and see how they all work together

☐ EVALUATION ESSAY—you look at the parts of something and compare it to a standard or an ideal

☐ WRITING ESSAY ANSWERS ON A TEST—you look at the test question, decide what the question is asking, and write an answer that is organized in a paragraph or a short essay

How many do you think you already know?_____

How many are you familiar with?_____

How many don't you know?_____

Overview of Academic Writing Tasks

Here is a list of academic writing tasks you probably will be expected to do in a North American college or university. By the time you finish this course, you will be able to do most of these tasks.

I.   Note-taking

   A. From reading texts and articles

   B. From interviews or speakers

II. Essays and Papers

   A. Writing from

      1. Facts you already know

      2. Facts you read about

      3. Facts you discover on your own

   B. Types of papers

      1. Essays

         a. Informal

         b. Formal

      2. Reports

      3. Research Papers

III. Examinations

   Answering test questions that require writing a paragraph or an essay.

Foundations of Academic Writing

In this course, you will learn the process for researching and writing successful academic papers. A process is something that you work through step-by-step. The process described in this book will give you a plan to follow in writing for your college courses, and should make you feel less anxiety. Two basic forms of academic writing are the essay and the research paper. An essay is a short piece of writing on a single subject. A research paper is a longer piece of writing that requires you to gather information from a number of sources and put it together so that you can inform or convince your reader of something. As you work through the activities in this book, you will have opportunities to master the academic writing process as you learn to gather information, take notes, and to write formal and informal essays and four research papers.

In this unit you will:

▼ Write a simple informal essay

▼ Learn the steps of the academic writing process

▼ Write an informal essay using the academic writing process

▼ Begin to understand the rules of research papers

You will also:

▼ Read model essays

▼ See how the steps of the academic writing process can be applied to a model

▼ Read models of simple research papers

▼ Learn basic guidelines for formal writing

Other skills you will practice are:

▼ Comparing the two essays you wrote

▼ Basic research using interviews

The Essay

INTRODUCTION

One of the most common writing assignments is the essay. An essay is a short piece of writing on a single subject. An essay can be as short as three to five paragraphs. Sometimes you choose the subject of an essay yourself, and sometimes the subject is assigned to you.

PART 1 *Essay Types*

There are two general types of essay, informal and formal. Study the definitions of both types.

Informal essays are written from your own experience and knowledge for a general audience. They are revised to improve content, organization, and mechanics (spelling, punctuation, sentence structure, and grammar). These essays are written in friendly, personal, everyday language and can be handwritten or typed.

Formal essays are written for an academic audience for a specific purpose. The language is formal. Like informal essays, they are revised many times to improve the content and organization and to correct errors in mechanics (spelling, punctuation, sentence structure, and grammar). They might use information from other sources. They are usually typed.

PART 2 *Essay Models*

When you prepare the final copy of an essay, you will want it to have a specific appearance. The appearance includes where you put your name, date, and class name on the paper. This information is called a heading. The appearance also includes the proper place for the title, capitalization of the title, the margins, and the font (or typewriter lettering) you use. In addition, academic papers are written or typed on only one side of a sheet of paper.

Following are handwritten and typed models of an essay called "Money, Money, Money! I Want More Money!" Look at them and identify the parts by answering these questions.

1. What information is found in the heading?
2. Where is the heading placed?
3. Where is the title? How is it capitalized?
4. How wide are the margins?
5. Why did the student skip lines in the body of the essay?

Handwritten model

> Rafael Delgado
> May 10, 1995
> College Writing
>
> Money, Money, Money! I Want More Money
>
> Is money that important? Many people are always concerned about
> getting as much money as they want, and sometimes they forget the real reason
> to have money. Then the desire to make more money becomes an obsession that
> can be difficult to stop. It is not bad to make money. As a matter of fact, we
> need it to survive in this world. We need money to buy food and pay for our
> rent, books, and entertainment. It is almost impossible to h

Typed model

Rafael Delgado
May 10, 1995
College Writing

Money, Money, Money! I Want More Money!

Is money that important? Many people are always concerned about getting as much money as they want, and sometimes they forget the real reason to have money. Then the desire to make more money becomes an obsession that can be difficult to stop. It is not bad to make money. As a matter of fact, we need it to survive in this world. We need money to buy food and pay for our rent, books, and entertainment. It is almost impossible to live without money. The problem is when money is the only thing we want.

Sometimes people get this obsession for money for the wrong reasons. They think that money will bring them better status, more friends, and more happiness. The question is, are they really friends and is that real happiness? Most of the time these friends and happiness last only as long as the money lasts. Real friends and happiness have so high a price that they cannot be bought with money.

Another problem with the obsession for money is that people forget to enjoy the "way through it." For example, sometimes students have their minds set on the graduation date or the day they have their diplomas in their hands. They forget that it is better to enjoy all the way, day by day, semester by semester. In the same way, people should enjoy making money and using it always, not as a final and big goal. For example, I can enjoy making $20,000 a year, then the next year $50,000, and then a million. I do not have to wait for happiness. I can enjoy the process.

Finally, the Lord says in the *New Testament* that it is not bad to make money if we have a wise purpose or if we use it to share with the people who need it. Since I do not have money, I share my time with others who need help, and this brings me satisfaction. In the same way, people who share their money to help others will find great satisfaction. It is not bad to have money, if you use it wisely.

Money is important. People should be concerned about getting money to live, but many important parts of life do not cost money. Therefore, money is not bad unless it is the only thing we want.

PART 3 *Assignment 1: Informal Essay*

▼ Write an informal essay following the information you have just studied. You have 30 minutes.

Write on the topic "The Importance of My College Major" or "The Importance of Learning English."

PRACTICE 1

Thinking about Assignment 1

▼ After you have finished Assignment 1, discuss with your classmates how you felt about the first writing assignment and how you fulfilled the assignment. Write short answers to these questions in your notebook.

1. How did you begin? (GETTING STARTED)
   - Did you wonder why this subject was given?
   - Did you think about who would read this essay?
   - What did you think the reader would want to know?
   - What did you think of that you decided the reader wouldn't want to know?

2. What did you do to plan before you began writing? (PREWRITING)
   - Did you plan in your head or on paper?
   - Did you write down any words or sentences?
   - How did you decide the first word?

3. What happened while you were actually writing? (ORGANIZING, REVISING, EDITING)
   - Did you want to rewrite some parts?
   - Were you trying to please the reader or yourself, the writer?
   - Was it easy to divide the paragraphs?
   - Did you think of starting some sentences with a clause or a prepositional phrase?
   - Did you have trouble with vocabulary, grammar, spelling, or punctuation?

4. What were you feeling?
   - Did you think that your work would be criticized?
   - Were you afraid, nervous, frustrated, unsure?
   - Was the subject a good one? Did you like it or dislike it?
   - Did you feel pressure from the 30-minute time limit?
   - Were you happy with what you wrote or did you want to start over again?

5. How does this assignment compare to other writings you have done?
   - Who read your other papers?
   - How many 30-minute essays have you written?
   - Have you written about this subject before?
   - Does the appearance of this essay look like other English essays?

6. What could help you to be less nervous and more organized? Write your ideas.

   _____

   _____

   _____

   _____

   _____

The Academic Writing Process

INTRODUCTION

Writing is a continuous process that ends with well-organized ideas on paper. A process means that you start at the beginning and go through several steps in a specific order. You will use the academic writing process in almost every paper you write for this course. Here are the steps in the academic writing process:

    I. GETTING STARTED

   II. PREWRITING

  III. GATHERING INFORMATION

  IV. ORGANIZING THE INFORMATION

   V. WRITING THE FIRST DRAFT

  VI. REVISING AND REWRITING

 VII. EDITING AND REWRITING

PART 1   *The Writing Process*

Now, here are more details for each of the steps. You will find out about all of these steps as you go through the book, and you will have many opportunities to practice these skills.

  I. GETTING STARTED

    A. Get the assignment

       1. Understand the assignment. (What should you do?)

   2. Understand the purpose. (Why is this necessary? What will you learn?)

   3. Identify the audience. (Who will read this? What do they want to know?)

   B. Choose a topic that you:

   1. are concerned about (What is important to you?)

   2. are interested in (What do you like? What topic excites you?)

   3. want to know more about (What would you like to learn?)

II. PREWRITING

   A. Discover all you know about the topic by using one or more of the following techniques:

   1. Make a list of everything you can think of about the topic (brainstorming).

   2. Ask yourself general questions and answer them, or ask more specific wh- questions (who, what, where, why, when, how).

   3. Use Venn diagrams or idea maps.

   4. Write (or talk) as fast as you can, saying anything that comes to your mind.

III. GATHERING INFORMATION

   A. Ask questions.

   B. Read articles.

   C. Choose information that explains the topic.

   D. Take notes on note cards.

IV. ORGANIZING INFORMATION

   A. Categorize and label information.

   B. Make a general plan (planning outline).

V. WRITING OR TYPING THE FIRST DRAFT

   A. Follow your planning outline.

   B. Write quickly.

VI. REVISING AND REWRITING

   A. Add more details, examples, explanations.

   B. Reorganize if necessary.

   C. Improve paragraphing.

   D. Change words or sentence structure.

VII. EDITING AND REWRITING

    A. Read your paper aloud.

    B. Correct errors in spelling, punctuation, and grammar.

(Repeat any steps as often as necessary.)

PART 2 *Model of the Academic Writing Process*

Study the model of the academic writing process. On the left is the process you have just studied. On the right is the work of a student who followed the steps to write an essay.

I. Getting Started

Topic: Why learning English is important to me

II. Prewriting

```
English
Jobs-    more opportunities, can find work
         anywhere
Money-   good home, enough food, good
         education for children
Influence-use my talents, teach my child
Travel-  English is universal language
```

III. Gathering Information That Will Help Clarify the Topic

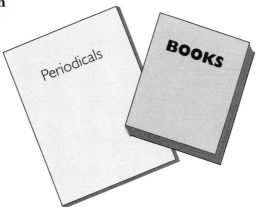

IV. Organizing Information

```
    I. Introduction
   II. Good jobs
       A. More opportunity
       B. Can work anywhere
       C. Higher pay
  III. Influence
       A. Teach children English
       B. Use English
          internationally
```

V. Writing or Typing the First Draft

Knowing English will be very benificial with me.

First I will be able to get a better job than if I didn't know English. I would be able for to find work somewhere I want to live. And I will get highter pay than peoples who don't know English.

Secondly, I will

VI. Revising and Rewriting

Knowing English will be very benificial with me. ⸲ since I am studying to become

~~First~~ *an engineer in an international business,* ~~I will be able to get a better job than if I didn't know English.~~ I
would be able for to find work ~~somewhere~~ *any*where
I want to live. *EX* And I will get highter pay than peoples who don't know English. *EX*

Secondly, I will

VII. Editing and Rewriting

Knowing English will be very ben*e*ficial *for* ~~with~~ me. First since I am studying to become an engineer in ⓐ international business, I will be able to find work anywhere I want to live. For example, there *is* ~~are~~ an international business in nearly every large city in my country so I can appl*ied* many places. Also I will get higher pay

VIII. Final Draft

> Knowing English will be very beneficial for me. First, since I am studying to become an engineer in a͜ international business, I will be able to find work anywhere I want to live. For example, there is an international business in nearly every large city in my country, so I can apply at many places. Also, I will get higher pay. My friend makes over $1,000 more each month than

PART 3 *Beginning Research with an Interview*

An important part of writing an academic paper is gathering information. Information most often comes from three sources:

* Facts you already know
* Facts you find from reading
* Facts you discover for yourself

The next writing assignment is an essay using information you discover for yourself. This information will be found by interviewing a classmate or another person approved by your teacher. Interviewing takes some skill. It really means that you help people talk about themselves by asking questions. You may want to practice on a friend or watch someone interview another person in your class or on television before you actually interview a person you don't know well.

Here are some tips for a successful interview:

1. Plan your interview questions to fit the time you have. Most North Americans will expect you to start and stop at the time you agree on.
2. Use your most polite and respectful language.
3. Stop asking about a subject if you see the person doesn't want to talk about that subject.
4. Be sure to ask many different types of questions and write down the answers in detailed notes. (The person may allow you to make a tape recording of the interview.)
5. Be prepared to ask many questions on the same topic if you find a subject that is especially interesting.

The audience, or readers, will be your classmates, so you will want to write about the most interesting information you can. To find such information, you need to ask questions that can be answered with more than "yes" or "no." The assignment for this unit includes some questions that may give you some topics to ask about.

PART 4   *Assignment 1: Using the Writing Process*

Now you are ready to follow the **writing process** as you do the next writing assignment for this unit.

I. GETTING STARTED

    A. Assignment: Write an essay about a classmate or another person.

    B. Choose a person to interview.

    C. Audience: Your classmates.

II. PREWRITING

    A. Write down everything you already know about the person. (If you don't know very much, you can make some guesses and ask about those in the interview.)

    B. Ask yourself what you and your audience might like to know about the person.

III. GATHERING MISSING INFORMATION   Due:

    A. Choose one or two questions from the list below to help you get started.

    B. Ask other questions that clarify what you hear.

    C. Be sure that you understand the answers.

    D. Write down the details of the answers (take notes).

    E. Ask more questions to get correct, interesting, and complete information.

Interview Questions

1. Can you remember a special birthday? What was special about it?

2. What sickness do you remember? Did you go to a hospital? What happened? How did you feel?

3. Have you ever had an accident? What happened?

4. What was the first money you ever earned? What did you do with it?

5. What is an event that you will always remember? What are the details?

6. In what ways are you just like one of your family members? (father/mother/sister/brother/cousin) How are you like this person?

7. Have you ever shocked or surprised anyone? What happened?

8. Have you ever been lucky? What happened? When?

9. What is the most valuable thing you have? Why is it valuable?

10. What is the funniest thing that ever happened to you? What happened?

Once you have completed the first three steps of the writing process, you are ready to organize your information. While you are doing that, you may need to ask the person you interviewed a few more questions.

IV. ORGANIZE THE INFORMATION

    A. Decide what information is most important.

    B. Decide what you will put first, second, third. Do you want to put the information in the time-order of life or will you organize it by interesting topic or idea?

    C. Number the information in your notes in the order you will write about it. (This is called a "planning" outline.)

V. WRITE THE FIRST DRAFT   Due:_____

    A. Write the essay about your partner.

    B. Be sure you follow your "planning" or "preliminary" outline.

VI. REVISE AND REWRITE   Due:_____

    A. Give your paper to the person you interviewed so that he or she can check the information for accuracy.

    B. Improve the content and organization of your sentences and paragraphs.

    C. Add more information to make the details clearer to the reader.

VII. EDIT AND REWRITE   Due:_____

    A. A classmate can also edit your paper for mechanical errors.

    B. Look for spelling, grammar, and punctuation mistakes.

    C. Prepare your paper to be presented in class.

PRACTICE 1

Reading an Essay from an Interview

The following essay was written from the notes taken from an interview of a Japanese student. Read it and discuss with the class the information that makes this essay interesting.

Yuji, the Brave Boy

Yuji is from Fukuoka, a city that is on the southern island of Japan. He is the youngest of three children in his family and has an older brother and sister. The family lives in a very large apartment building.

Yuji has two goals in his life. The first one is to become a police officer like his grandfather. When he was young, he enjoyed hearing the many "cop" stories his grandfather used to tell him. Also, he often went to the station and asked the other officers questions about what they do.

His second goal is to have a happy family like his own family. His parents have worked hard to provide their children with a good education and a nice home. They also have shown a lot of love and affection to the family. This is what Yuji wants.

When Yuji was a small boy, he enjoyed trains, and he often went to play on the railroad crossing near his home in the country. He loved to play on the tracks, swing on the crossing gates, see the blinking red lights, and hear the bell.

One day when he was playing on the crossing, he got his foot caught between the track and the roadbed. He pulled and pulled, but he could not get his foot unstuck! Suddenly the red lights began to blink, the bell began to sound, and the crossing gates began to come down. He pulled and pulled! Finally his foot came out of his shoe, and he ran from the crossing. Within 30 seconds the train roared past! Later, when he went back to get his shoe, it was smashed and very dirty. When his mother asked him why his one shoe was dirty, he said that he had been kicking dirt with that foot. To this day she does not know that her little son was almost killed by a train!

Because of his good luck, Yuji is alive and is now studying English in the United States.

PRACTICE 2

Comparing Writing Assignments 1 and 2

Even though the first two writing assignments of this chapter were both essays, they were different in many important ways. In writing assignment 1, you were given a title and a time limit. In writing assignment 2, you followed the academic writing process.

▼ In small groups or pairs, compare the two essay assignments.

▼ Answer the following questions and then write down the answers that you all agree on.

1. How was 1 different from 2?

_____

_____

_____

_____

2. In what ways was 1 easier than 2?

_____

_____

_____

_____

3. In what ways was 2 easier than 1?

_____

_____

_____

_____

4. Which one had more problems with:

   a.   flow of ideas?   1   2

   b.   organization?   1   2

   c.   not enough details?   1   2

   d.   word choice?   1   2

   e.   grammar?   1   2

   f.   division of paragraphs?   1   2

   g.   selection of details?   1   2

5. In your own mind, who was your audience when you wrote 2?

   _____

   _____

   _____

   _____

6. Is prewriting important to you? Why or why not?

   _____

   _____

   _____

   _____

7. Is revising, editing, and rewriting several times important to you? Why
   or why not?

   _____

   _____

   _____

   _____

The Research Paper

CHAPTER 3

INTRODUCTION

You will write four research papers in this course. The first three papers will be short as you learn particular writing and research skills. The fourth paper will be longer and will include all the elements of a good research paper.

There are different styles (or rules) that research papers must follow. It is important to follow these rules when you write formal papers. This text uses the American Psychological Association (APA) style guidelines for writing all papers.

PART 1 *Research Paper Model*

Look at the following example on pages 18 to 25 of a research paper in APA style. As you examine the paper, write your own answers to these questions.

1. How is information on the title page arranged?
    - What is a title page for?

    _____

    _____

    _____

    _____

2. What is an abstract?

    _____

    _____

    _____

    _____

3. What is the heading in the upper right-hand corner of each page?

    ● Why is this necessary?

    _____

    _____

    _____

    _____

4. What do you see in the spacing of the lines and the margins in the paper?

    ● Why do you find different margins within the paper?

    _____

    _____

    _____

    _____

5. What do you find between the parentheses ( )?

    ● What is this information for?

    _____

    _____

    _____

    _____

6. What are some of the formal writing elements in the paper?

    ● Does it have a formal introduction?

    _____

    ● How many paragraphs does it have?

    _____

    ● Does it have a formal conclusion?

    _____

7. What other characteristics do you notice?

    _____

    _____

    _____

    _____

The Effects of Television Violence on Children

Rafael Delgado

Brigham Young University

The Effects of Television

2

Abstract

From recent studies we know that violent television programs do affect children's behavior. They promote imitative play including violence and obscene language, demonstrate that violence is the key to power and problem-solving, and even push children to commit crime. In addition, TV can distort feelings and portray a frightening world. Parents can help change the influence of the constant effect of television violence.

The Effects of Television

3

Outline

I.   Introduction

Thesis statement: violent TV programs affect children's behavior.

II.   Promote violent imitative play

III.   Teach obscene language

IV.   Demonstrate that violence is power

V.   Teach that violence solves problems

VI.   Encourage aggressive behavior

VII. Distort reality

VIII. Portray a frightening world

IX.   Conclusion

The Effects of Television Violence on Children

"Television is not reflecting the world, but the world is reflecting television" (Brady, 1992, p. 50). Television is the widespread medium that brings violence to our youngsters and, as a matter of fact, it is not hard to imagine how many ways TV violence affects children. But it is difficult to determine the level of responsibility television has for their aggressive behavior. Some researchers say that the relationship is direct, while others maintain that children copy it from their home environment. However, most parents who are really concerned about the increase of violence in their children are the ones who do not have violent behavior in their homes. They ask themselves, "Where is the child learning this, if we are not giving him or her the example?" From recent studies we know that violent television programs do affect children's behavior.

Television causes children to change their creative spirit for an imitative desire that may include violent behavior. They learn to dress, act, and even think like their TV idols. For example, as a child, I used to act, talk, and even run as the "Bionic Man." I always tried to copy and learn from him as much as I could. In this same way, a child may choose a violent character and think of this character as himself, and then want to learn and copy his or her violent thoughts and ideas. In addition, the programs themselves promote imitative play by selling rights to make program toys. Some of these toys are violent characters. Together, the child with the specially designed toy will try to imitate the TV characters as best as possible. In addition, we hear children saying, "Let's play war." Is that a real game? Can they really have fun? They don't know what war really is. They just have the smooth idea television gives them about war and they want to imitate what they have seen.

Along with imitative play, violent programs can teach children to use bad language. It is very common to find television programs and movies with a large portion of obscene words. A child who is trying to imitate a character will also imitate his or her vocabulary without analyzing if it is good or bad. For example, my aunt forbade my three-year-old cousin to watch the TV cartoon "The Simpsons" because he was learning to talk to older people in a disrespectful manner, as Bart Simpson does.

Furthermore, "Television depicts violence as the key to power. It is the way power is obtained and how it is exercised" (Schwartzberg, 1987, p. 102) When he was asked why he liked Hulk Hogan, a child answered: "... because he hurts people, and then they do what he wants" (p. 102). Children learn that violence is the best way to get power. There are thousands of TV programs that show how easy it is to get power through cheating, lying, hurting, and even killing people. This situation is shown not only in TV movies, but also very often in cartoons, where it is easier to present violence as the way to get power. "When you hurt people, you get what you want" is the message TV shows may project.

As well as teaching violence as power, TV also presents violence as the only way to solve problems. Children see on TV how, time after time, violence brings solutions to problems. "If they see characters they enjoy watching using violence to solve problems, they will view violence as an acceptable problem-solving method" (Schwartzberg, 1987, p. 104). For example, a preschool teacher, Tony Harrison, said "... the sound of a three-year-old boy yelling 'Cowabunga' is a war cry that can unleash chaos in the classroom. Suddenly, we are faced with a little gang of Ninjas trying to kick each other in the face" (Brady, 1992, p. 50). Children love these characters and the way they solve problems (usually violently). Even though the main purpose of a TV show may not be to teach violent solutions, children who take these heroes as examples undoubtedly will try the same methods to solve their problems.

It is worrisome when children use violence to solve their problems, but even more when they develop aggressive and hostile behavior just because they have seen it on TV. Most of the research agrees that violent TV programs can cause violent behavior to develop in all people and mainly in children. Brady (1992) says that what children see doesn't just encourage children to be violent, but even teaches them a particular technique. For example,

In October, 1989, two Burlington, Ontario, teenagers, Steven Olah, who was 18 at the time, and James Ruston, then 17, murdered a 44-year-old department store executive in a gas station as part of a bungled robbery. They killed the man by hitting him over the head more than thirty times with a fire extinguisher. During their trial on charges of first-degree murder, Olah told the court that the two

The Effects of Television

6

youths thought they could knock the victim unconscious with a couple of blows. "We have seen it in the movies all the time," Olah testified. "You hit him once and down he goes" (Jenish, 1992, p. 42).

Another effect of television on children is the distortion it creates about life. TV shows children just one part of life. For example, there is a big difference between watching a basketball game on the court and watching it on TV. While attending the game, the emotions of the crowd and the players add excitement, noise, and personal involvement. Television takes away a lot of the emotion of the game. Someone else decides what part of the game will be seen and how it will be interpreted. In the same way, television projects a cold idea of violence. It seems as if there is no pain, sadness, or any of those real and strong feelings around crimes. Children, not seeing these real feelings, are not afraid of doing the same acts as on television. In addition, Schwartzberg explains that most children, even as late as third grade, have a hard time deciding what "real" means...(1987, p. 104). Jenish (1992) relates that even 15-year-olds can have this problem. Sharon Richardson now makes her 15-year-old son, Graham, turn off violent programs. She says, "Once Graham told me it wasn't violent. It was just clean shooting. He thinks that's not violence, because he saw no pain. I said, 'Wait a minute. You just saw people shot. Their lives were ended.' And he answered, 'But there was no suffering'" (Jenish, 1992, p. 41). The prospect that someday a generation of children like this will have to face the cold world with their lack of feelings is quite discomforting.

Finally, television violence can bring to children the idea of a frightening world. Every day they can see threatening acts on television. Television programs have affected the eleven-year-old daughter of Donald Mills because of some of the crimes she has seen against women on TV. She will not stay home alone and she is unusually cautious and frightened about being female (Jenish,1992).

In conclusion, from television children may learn these things about violence: it teaches that the world is frightening; it distorts the reality of feeling; it is a way to get power and solve problems; and it is something to be imitated in language and behavior. The real problem is that violence on television does not appear in just some TV shows, but is in many television presentations, such as advertisements, movies, soap operas, previews and cartoons. More than just being concerned, parents should be very careful of the kind of TV programs their children are watching so they can guide them. This guidance includes talking to their children about violent TV programs, watching the programs with them, and explaining the real effects of the violent actions seen on the programs. This way the children will learn to handle an influence that will always be around them.

The Effects of Television

8

References

Brady, D. (1992, December). The power of 'cowabunga'. <u>Maclean's</u>,
    p. 50.

Jenish, D. (1992, December). Prime-Time violence. <u>Maclean's</u>,
    pp. 40-44.

Katz, L. (1991, January). As they grow. <u>Parents</u>, p. 113.

Schwartzberg, N. (1987, June). What TV does to kids. <u>Parents</u>,
    pp. 100-104.

Silver, M. (1993, April). Troubling TV ads. <u>US News & World Report</u>,
    p. 65.

PART 2 *Formal Writing Guidelines*

1. Style guidelines

   - Papers should carefully follow the style guidelines expected. Some common academic style guidelines are:

     APA (American Psychological Association)

     MLA (Modern Language Association)

     Turabian

     Campbell, Ballou, and Slade

     This book uses APA style guidelines.

2. Author's position

   - The total paper is considered to be the work of the writer. You don't have to say "I think" or "My opinion is" in the paper.

   - The position of the author is usually shown in the thesis statement.

3. Traditional formality

   - Traditional formal writing does not use *I* or *we* in the body of the paper. This idea is changing, but not all audiences will accept these changes.

   - Some college subjects traditionally require using the passive sentence form in your writing. In other subjects, the active form of the sentence is preferred. Find out what your audience (such as your teacher) traditionally expects before you write the paper.

   - Starting a sentence with *And* is less formal. It should be avoided.

   - Asking the reader questions in your paper is more conversational and, therefore, less formal.

4. Logic

   - Using traditional formal elements in your paper helps readers see your logic in the way they have come to expect.

   - Words and phrases that show the relationship of one idea to another help the reader see connections between ideas and understand your reasoning.

5. Physical appearance

   - Typed papers that carefully follow all the required style rules receive higher grades.

   - Be conservative when typing. Use a standard font (or typewriter letters) for the title page and the paper. Do not write in all capital, italicized, or bold letters.

   - Type only on one side of the sheet of paper.

   - Place papers neatly in order in three-hole or paper-grip folders with your name easily seen on the front of the folders. Do not hand in loose papers.

Writing A Summary

A summary is a short written statement of the main ideas or the most important facts in a larger work. Summarizing is often required in courses such as business, literature, and science. It can help you recognize main ideas and important facts, a skill that will help you select information for your research papers. Therefore, knowing how to write a good summary is the first important step in writing successful academic papers.

In this unit you will:

▼ write a summary of a paragraph

▼ write a summary of an entire essay and article

▼ write a summary using information from more than one source

You will also learn to:

▼ find main ideas and important facts

▼ change that information into your own words (paraphrase)

▼ organize the information

▼ make outlines

▼ write short summaries from outlines

▼ combine information from two articles into a summary report

Other skills you will practice are:

▼ using encyclopedias at the library

▼ writing bibliographic references

▼ making marginal notes

Main Ideas

MAIN IDEA

↑

Details
Facts
Examples

In academic writing, almost every paragraph has a main idea. All of the sentences in the paragraph will give the reader some details about the main idea. The details can be facts, descriptions, examples, or experiences showing important or interesting information to help the reader understand the main idea.

The main idea of a paragraph is supported by details, facts, and examples. The relationship is shown in the diagram on the left.

The overall topic, or main idea, of an entire article has the same relationship to all the main ideas in the paragraphs, which are then supported by details. These layered relationships might look like this:

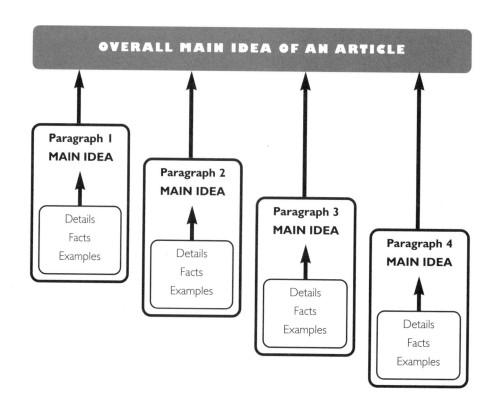

P A R T 1 *Finding Main Ideas*

In most academic writing the main idea of the paragraph is found in the first sentence. This sentence is called the topic sentence.

Example:

The childhood of the British queen, Queen Elizabeth I, was quite difficult. First of all, her father, King Henry VIII, wanted a son and eventually killed her mother because she couldn't give him a male heir. Her father married six times. He divorced two wives, beheaded two, one died giving birth to his only son, and one survived him. When Mary, Elizabeth's half sister, became queen, she put Elizabeth in prison because she was jealous of her. Elizabeth certainly did not have a normal childhood.

The main idea is found in the topic sentence and is about the difficult childhood of Queen Elizabeth I. The rest of the paragraph gives details to show how difficult it was for her.

The main idea can occur in other places in a paragraph or can be inferred. Part 4 in this chapter will help you understand other variations.

PRACTICE 1

Finding Main Ideas

▼ Read paragraph 1, written by a student.

▼ Underline the sentence/sentences that state the main idea.

▼ Write the main idea in your own words on the line below. Do not copy the exact sentence.

Paragraph 1

When I teach Japanese to Americans, I'll teach them three kinds of greetings. The first one is a general group of greetings like *konnichiwa, ohayo, konbanwa, oyasumi,* and *genki?* These mean "hello," "good morning," "good evening," and "how are you?" They are used the same way as in English. The second group is used when you eat. *Itadakimasu* is used before eating a meal, and *gochisousama* is used after eating. These are greetings of thanks for the meal like a prayer. The last group is used when we leave the house or come home. When we leave the house, we say *ittekimasu,* and when we come home, we say *tadaima.* These words let the family know if we are home or not. By using these greetings at home, we will be able to have good communication.

(Hitomi Shimada—Japan)

Main Idea:

_____

_____

Now find the main idea of paragraph 2 on your own. Follow the instructions above.

Paragraph 2

> A hairpin in ancient China was a very important ornament for a female. The kind of hairpin told about the female wearing it. If she were rich, the hairpin would be made of silver or gold. It would be very colorful, also. If she were not rich, then the hairpin would be made of wood or copper and be simple in style. But for women in ancient China, what she was was more important than what she had. I think that is the same rule nowadays.
>
> *(Yuchen Kuang—Taiwan)*

Main idea:

_____

_____

PART 2 *Writing Main Ideas*

Look at the following paragraph, which is missing the topic sentence. Find the main idea by reading through the details carefully.

> The shaking of the earth causes gas lines to break, and huge fires are caused that destroy entire buildings. These fires can cause explosions of other areas as well. In addition, freeway structures collapse, and streets and highways are twisted and broken. Sometimes when an earthquake hits during high traffic hours, hundreds of people are killed in their cars. Furthermore, houses crumble and slide down hills, they collapse on the people inside, or they disappear in huge cracks in the earth. In seconds, people die, become homeless, or are trapped under fallen structures. The injuries to people and the damage to property cost millions.

The topic of this paragraph is "the damage that earthquakes cause." Therefore, a good topic sentence might be "Earthquakes are very destructive" or "The damage caused by earthquakes is unbelievable."

PRACTICE 2

Writing/Identifying Main Ideas

▼ Read the following paragraphs written by a student. The main ideas are not stated.

▼ Look carefully at the details.

▼ Write the main idea on the line after the paragraph.

Paragraph 1

> When I was a child, I couldn't sleep without the light because I was very scared when I thought about a ghost at night. My mother said that there was no ghost, so I had to switch off the light. In addition, I hated to go into a dark haunted house in a recreation park. My friends wanted me to go inside because they enjoyed frightening me. The make-believe bodies in the haunted house didn't bother me. I'm more afraid of a place that is very dark inside.
>
> *(Mieko Tani—Japan)*

Main idea:

_____

Paragraph 2

> First, write a letter to the admissions office and ask for some information about the university. For example, "How much is the tuition?" or "How many students do you have?" and so on. You can also ask for an application form. Next, fill out the application form with your personal information. You should also collect the documents that are required, such as your transcript and TOEFL score (only for international students). Finally, send in your application form and the other documents. An important point is that you get the information there before the deadline. After that, you just wait for their reply letter. If you follow these steps, you can easily apply to a university by yourself.
>
> *(Mieko Tani—Japan)*

Main idea:

_____

PART 3 *Summarizing Main Ideas of an Essay*

Now you are ready to look for main ideas in an essay and write a summary of those ideas. The skill of recognizing main ideas in written material will help you in your studies. Not only will you be able to summarize effectively, but you will also understand and remember the material you read more easily.

The beginning and ending paragraphs of an essay are called the introduction and the conclusion. In academic writing they are usually not organized in the same way as a paragraph, but reading them will help you find the overall idea of the entire essay.

Steps for Summarizing
Main Ideas

Step 1

▼ Read the following essay once quickly.

▼ Carefully reread and look for main ideas as you read.

▼ Write the main ideas of paragraphs 2, 3, 4, and 5 in different words in the left margin.

▼ Discuss your ideas with the class.

Causes of Youth Suicide

(Introduction) 1.   Many more young people die of suicide than of cancer. The word *suicide* is defined as "a conscious act of self-induced annihilation" (Schneidman, 1985, p. 203). Many young people have experiences that make them feel as if they want to die. They feel that they need to escape this situation and they choose suicide.

2.   One cause of suicide is the death of a parent. Because the death of a parent occurs suddenly and mysteriously, it makes the children's mental pain unbearable. Children feel loneliness, loss of love, and the loss of belonging to someone. Often they feel cheated. They may choose death to reunite with their parents (Pfeffer, 1986).

3.   Another reason is alienation from the family (Tembly, 1961). Alienation may be caused because the parents control too much, or ignore the children, or by the loss of a parent through separation or divorce. When children don't feel how much their parents love them or care for them, many children will smoke or use drugs or try other antisocial behavior to get the attention they need from their parents. When this fails, they may try suicide.

4.   Rejection in love causes unbearable disappointment, not to mention frustration and depression, and sometimes leads to suicide. A young girl named Leslie, who attempted suicide, said, "My boyfriend called and said it was all over. . . . There was so much pain I had to get away from it. . . . No one wanted me." (Crook, 1989, pp. 60–61). My high school classmate attempted suicide because she felt she couldn't live without her boyfriend. After several years, she got married to a different man. Later she said, "I don't know why I tried suicide for such a silly guy." When her attempt at suicide occurred, she was not mature. But love seems a serious thing at any age, and the rejection of that love hurts.

5.   Sometimes youths try suicide because of academic pressure. Seiden (1966) says that the suicide rate among college students is significantly higher than among youths not in college, especially in Japan. In Japan, an educational background affects future goals completely. If students graduate from a good university, they can get good jobs; otherwise, they can't. I felt as if my life was over when I failed to get into a good university in Japan. However, at that time my parents encouraged me to find another way to improve myself. Luckily, they saw what I needed and gave me their support, so I didn't attempt suicide. However, in the United States there is also a

lot of pressure from society to enter a good university. "The situation [in the U.S.A.] ominously resembles a suicidal problem that prevails among the youth of Japan . . . [where] there are tremendous pressures to attend college, and those students who fail to gain entrance frequently turn to suicide as a solution to their dilemmas" (Sieden, 1966, p. 399).

(Conclusion) 6.   Youths often kill themselves because of the death of a parent, alienation, rejection, and academic pressures. There would be fewer suicides if there were more family support and less pressure from society. Societal pressure is needed, but not to the extent that the children feel there is no way out of a situation except through death. So adults really need to care about their children to protect them from suicide.

(Haruko Fujibayashi—Japan)

References

Crook, M. (1989). Teenagers talk about suicide. Toronto: N. C. Press Ltd.

Pfeffer, C. (1986). The suicidal child. New York: The Guilford Press.

Schneidman, E. (1985). Definition of suicide. New York: John Wiley & Sons.

Seiden, R. (1966). Campus tragedy: Study of student suicide. Journal of Abnormal Psychology, 71(6), 389–399.

Tembly, W. (1961). Emotional problems of the student. New York: Appleton-Century-Crofts.

Step 2

Write your ideas in the blanks below.

Main idea of paragraph 2:

_____

_____

Main idea of paragraph 3:

_____

Main idea of paragraph 4:

_____

Main idea of paragraph 5:

_____

Overall idea of the entire essay:

_____

_____

Step 3

▼ In your notebook, write a short summary of this essay.

▼ Use only the information from step 2.

▼ Write the overall idea of the entire essay first.

▼ Do not look back at the essay!

▼ Remember to write the proper heading on your paper.

PRACTICE 3

Summarizing Main Ideas of an Essay

▼ Read the model essay in Unit One (p. 4) entitled "Money, Money, Money! I Want More Money!"

▼ Write the main idea of each paragraph in the margin as you understand it.

▼ Do not copy!

▼ Write the main idea of the entire essay.

▼ Starting with the overall main idea, write a summary.

PART 4 *Hidden Main Ideas*

Not all academic paragraphs have the main idea in the first sentence. This is especially true with personal topics and informal writing. However, it is never incorrect in academic style to write the topic and main idea in the first sentence.

You can also find the main ideas:

● in the first two sentences. Often the first sentence introduces the main idea and the second sentence is more specific.

● in the answer to a question.

● at the end of a paragraph.

Sometimes the main idea is not directly stated. This is an indirect or hidden main idea. This does not mean there is not a purpose for the paragraph. It is just that the purpose, or main idea, is found by adding up the meaning of the supporting details in the sentences. In this case, the reader must read all of the paragraph and then think about what the paragraph means.

To illustrate, look carefully at this paragraph.

When I was a young, impatient little girl, I ruined one of my Christmases. This particular Christmas, each day, as the "big day" approached, I would check the packages under and in the Christmas tree to see which ones were mine. But each day I counted only one present for me. It was a little white envelope with my name on it in the branches of the tree. As the days went by, my curiosity became stronger. Soon I began to carefully open the envelope a little each day. Finally I got it open enough to see that it was a year's subscription to Donald Duck comic books, which

I loved. When Christmas Day arrived, I tried to act surprised when I "opened" my gift, but I only felt that I had taken the joy out of Christmas because of my impatience.

The purpose, or main idea, of this paragraph is how a little girl learned patience. The main idea is found by looking at the meaning of all the sentences. The rest of the paragraph gives the details about the experience.

P R A C T I C E　4

Finding Hidden
Main Ideas

▼ Read the student essay quickly.

▼ Carefully consider each paragraph to find the main idea.

▼ Write the main idea in your own words in the left margin.

Hypocrite

When I was a little boy, my mother's advice was to wait for the light to turn green before I crossed the street and to cross always at the corner. This I always did. I was positive that I would get mashed like a potato if I even so much as stepped a foot off the sidewalk while the light was red. However, when we were downtown together, I followed my mother, who was constantly going in and out of moving traffic and pulling me with her. So, after a while, I followed the example and not the advice.

Like my mother, my father told me never to lie, cheat, or steal. I remember an intense humiliation on my birthday. I was only eight years old. I received a spanking for stealing three dimes from the windowsill where they had been left from my uncle's visit. It was not until after several punishments for lying that I began to follow my parents' recommendation. Even so, I knew, in time, that they lied to me on several occasions and even to each other.

As I grew up, I began to see the hypocrisy in what my parents said and what they did. In my late teens, I saw hypocrisy in my friends' families, in my school, and in the government. Then I realized that my parents were just human. They were that way, people were that way, so the world is that way. Hypocrisy is a part of life.

(Oscar Flores—Central America)

To summarize, you can find the main idea in four ways:

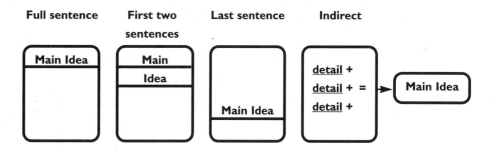

The Summarizing Process

In this chapter you will look more closely at the details in a paragraph. You will learn how to pick out important facts that you will use in writing a summary of an article.

PART 1 *Writing Important Facts as Marginal Notes*

Most of the information that you read for your research papers will be in the form of articles in periodicals or chapters from books. Sometimes you might even read information on microfiche or microfilm. Whenever possible, you will need to make a photocopy of the material so you can underline or highlight important facts as you read. You may also want to write words in the margin that state the main ideas and point to the facts. These words and phrases in the margins are called *marginal notes*.

The following paragraph is from a student paper. Notice the underlined information and the marginal notes. Marginal notes not only help you write summaries, but they also help you find information that you might need later. Notice that the marginal notes are words and phrases, not complete sentences.

Paragraph using marginal notes

Marginal notes on facts

There are <u>three</u> ways that my grandfather is different from me. First, he was a Chinese <u>doctor</u> when he lived in China. I am an <u>engineer.</u> In addition, old-fashioned Chinese men used to marry more than one woman. My grandfather also had <u>two wives</u> in his life; however, I just married this year. I only, and just only, have <u>my wife</u> in my life. Moreover, my grandfather loved <u>poems.</u> On the contrary, I like <u>formulas and equations.</u> Therefore, you can see the differences between us.

<u>occupations</u>
doctor
engineer

<u>marriages</u>
two wives
one wife

<u>interests</u>
poems
equations, formulas

(Arthur Chung—Taiwan)

The main idea of this paragraph is that Arthur and his grandfather are different. The facts are found in their occupations, their marriages, and their interests. The important facts that support this main idea could be shown this way:

<u>Occupations</u>
Grandfather—doctor
Arthur—engineer

<u>Marriages</u>
Grandfather—two wives
Arthur—one wife

<u>Interests</u>
Grandfather—poems
Arthur—formulas, equations

PRACTICE 1

Writing a Short Summary Statement

▼ In your notebook, write a short statement that uses only the marginal notes.

▼ Do not look at the original paragraph.

▼ Share your statement with the class or a classmate.

PRACTICE 2

Finding the Important Facts

Sometimes it is difficult to decide what is an important fact and what is not. Since an important fact is one that supports a main idea, you need to determine what the main idea is. You might look for clues in the topic sentences, in the introduction, and in the conclusion. Or as you read the article, the main idea will begin to form in your mind. When you recognize the main idea, the important facts that support it are easier to find.

▼ Read the following articles.

▼ Underline the important facts and write marginal notes.

▼ Write the main idea below each article.

Example 1 (Biography)

Thomas Alva Edison

For 60 years Thomas Alva Edison was the world's leading inventor. Few people realized how hard Edison worked, often 20 hours a day, and that most of his inventions were the results of hundreds of experiments. He patented over a thousand inventions that changed our way of living, including the mimeograph machine, wax wrapping paper, and improvements of the telegraph and telephone. He designed the central power station that became the model for the first public electric plant in New York City, providing electric power for thousands of homes and businesses. Edison was one of the earliest inventors of the motion picture machines. He also perfected the electric motor, which made streetcars and electric trains possible. However, his most important invention was the electric light. Yet, amid all his fame, Edison remained a modest man. His motto was: "I find what the world needs; then I go ahead and try to invent it." He never considered himself a brilliant man and once remarked that genius was "two per cent inspiration and ninety-eight percent perspiration."

(United States Information Agency. Used by permission.)

Main idea:

_____

_____

Example 2 (History)

Jane Addams

Following the American Civil War, immigrants filled the ships from the Old World and poured into the United States. With the immigrants also came problems for Chicago. The city grew too fast. Its population almost doubled in the 1880s. Many of its people were poor, miserable, and ignorant of the ways of the New World. They were crowded into small rooms in dark and dirty buildings. Working conditions were bad, and safety measures practically did not exist.

At first, no one seemed to care about these poor conditions. Then, one young woman who did care appeared on the scene. She was Jane Addams, 29 years old, well educated and from a wealthy, cultured family. She founded a social center in Chicago, the famous Hull House, which became a model for similar centers throughout the country. Miss Addams recognized that Hull House could not deal with these problems on a large scale, but that the federal or state governments could. Therefore, she and her Hull House workers began to fight for new social legislation. In every field of social action—child labor, problems of youth, women's rights, industrial medicine, and safety—she helped lead the struggle for a better way of life.

(United States Information Agency. Used by permission.)

Main idea:

_____

_____

P A R T 2 *Summarizing a Biography*

To learn how to summarize information, you will be using two biographies: Article 1 about Stephen Crane and Article 2 about Abraham Lincoln. Article 1 will be used to introduce the steps to summary writing. Article 2 will be used to practice those steps.

Read Article 1 and discuss the main ideas with the class.

Article 1

Father of Modern American Fiction

Stephen Crane is probably best known for his American Civil War novel, *The Red Badge of Courage,* a story of the reactions of an inexperienced soldier to the horrors of war. He, however, was chiefly a writer of short stories, the most noteworthy of which are "The Blue Hotel," "The Bride Comes to Yellow Sky," and "The Open Boat."

Crane lived during the last three decades of the nineteenth century and, like many artists of his time, rejected traditional romantic themes and wrote about what he saw around him in the most realistic terms—the cruel and violent, as well as the gentle and humorous.

Robert E. Spiller, one of America's leading literary historians, believes that modern American fiction was born with Stephen Crane's work. Though the total volume of his work may be too slender to qualify him as a first-rate writer, he is still an important figure in the American fiction of the nineteenth century.

Son of a Methodist minister, Crane was born on November 1, 1871, in Newark, New Jersey, the youngest of fourteen children. His childhood was a happy one. In school, he was more interested in baseball than in his studies, and at one time he considered becoming a professional ball player. But the career of a writer was his natural choice, and after two years of college, he went to New York to write. There he lived for five hard years, enduring much illness and achieving no success in his work.

In New York, Crane made a small amount of money by writing for newspapers, but his real writing at this time was his first novel, *Maggie: A Girl of the Streets.* Unlike other writers who sentimentalized or moralized about what they saw, Crane accurately told of the cruelty and poverty of city life. He published *Maggie* at his own expense, but it did not sell well. At that time, the story was considered so shockingly realistic that the publisher refused to identify himself with the book.

Meanwhile, half-starved and often ill, Crane continued to write. In 1893, he completed *The Red Badge of Courage.* He was only 22 years old. It was published two years later and quickly became a best-seller. Suddenly Crane found himself a famous young man. Unfortunately, he made only $100 from the book.

Nevertheless, having won fame with a military book, Crane spent his life thereafter reporting wars. Under the mistaken notion that only those who have experienced an event can become its interpreters, he expended himself in search of experience. He deliberately chose to get as close to life as possible. He traveled through the American West. He was a war correspondent in the Spanish-American and Greco-Turkish Wars. But what interested Crane more than the events, was the people—how they reacted to the situations in which they found themselves.

On one occasion, to experience the real thing, he stood all night in a blizzard in order to write the story "Men in the Storm." Out of his travels across the Western prairies, he wrote "The Blue Hotel" and "The Bride Comes to Yellow Sky." Both stories reveal the primitiveness that still existed among people in the "wilder" parts of the American West, and both end on a note of irony—a characteristic device of Crane's writing.

In 1896, seeking more experiences, Crane went to Florida and sailed on a small steamer carrying guns for the insurrectionists in Cuba. The steamer sank early in the voyage, and for 50 hours, Crane and a group of other men tossed about in a stormy sea in a lifeboat. From this experience, Crane wrote the story, "The Open Boat," which is considered by some of his critics as the finest piece of its kind. In no other story does Crane understand fear so clearly or express it so effectively. It is characteristic of his writing that he chose to record the meaning of life in moments of crisis. In his instinctive balance between reality and imagination, he achieved his superb art.

Returning to Florida after the shipwreck, Crane was welcomed by Cora Taylor, whom he had met not long before. The Boston-born daughter of a minor painter, she was five years older than Crane and had been twice married. She fell in love with him, and he became the center of her life.

Together they went to Greece where Crane, on assignment from British and American periodicals, reported on the war between Greece and Turkey. His shipwreck experience, however, had ruined his health and he contracted tuberculosis.

Too ill to stay in Greece, Crane went with Cora to England. However, with the start of the Spanish-American War in 1898, Crane once again became eager for new experiences. He accepted an offer to go to Cuba as a highly paid correspondent for a New York newspaper. Despite his bad health, he was a tireless reporter of the war. He wrote not so much of military maneuvers as of soldiers and their reactions in battle.

After returning to New York, Crane and Cora again retired to England. There he continued to write, using up his fast-ebbing strength. But tuberculosis advanced upon him. Desperately, he and Cora went to a health resort in Germany, but it was too late. There on June 5, 1900, Stephen Crane died. He was less than 29 years old.

Though Crane's writing career ended prematurely, his prolific output in those few short years had a profound influence on American literature. All his writing cannot, of course, be considered equally good. But Crane's vivid impressions of life, his keen insight, his fine distinctive style, colorful and forceful, provided a pattern for later writers. He gave the naturalistic novel and short story the characteristic form which was later used by Ernest Hemingway, William Faulkner, John Steinbeck, and a host of others.

United States Information Agency. Used by permission.

Steps for Summarizing
Important Facts

Step 1: Selecting important facts in Article 1

▼ Read the article again and underline the important facts.

▼ Write marginal notes to point to the facts.

▼ Compare your work to a classmate's. Ask:

  ● Did I underline too much?

  ● Did I miss some important points?

  ● Did I use only one word or a short phrase in the margins?

  ● Is my work different because my idea of what is important is different?

  ● Do I want to keep, add, or change some things?

Step 2: Outlining important facts

Once you have found the main ideas and the most important facts, you are ready to organize the information in an outline form. An outline will help you group the facts according to the main ideas you found.

Each part of an outline has a specific function. Look carefully at the outline model below. Answer these questions as you examine the parts of the outline:

1. In which part would a main idea be written?

2. In which part would a fact be written?

Outline model

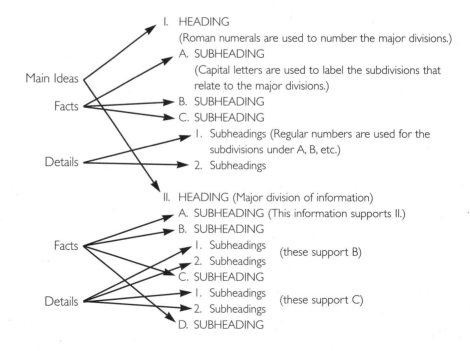

Main Ideas

Facts

Details

I. HEADING
    (Roman numerals are used to number the major divisions.)
A. SUBHEADING
    (Capital letters are used to label the subdivisions that relate to the major divisions.)
B. SUBHEADING
C. SUBHEADING
    1. Subheadings (Regular numbers are used for the subdivisions under A, B, etc.)
    2. Subheadings

II. HEADING (Major division of information)
A. SUBHEADING (This information supports II.)
B. SUBHEADING
    1. Subheadings
    2. Subheadings   (these support B)
C. SUBHEADING
    1. Subheadings
    2. Subheadings   (these support C)
D. SUBHEADING

Facts

Details

Example outline

WEATHER IN PROVO, UTAH
I. Summer
   A. Hot—100 degrees
   B. Thunderstorms
      1. Thunder
      2. Lightning
      3. Sudden and fast rain

II. Winter
   A. Short days
   B. Cold
      1. Below 32° F during the day
      2. Below 0° F during the night
   C. Snow
      1. Three to four feet
      2. Storms come mostly at night
   D. Fog

PRACTICE 3

Organizing the ideas and facts in Article 1

▼ Work in small groups. Each group will organize the main ideas and facts from the Stephen Crane article, "Father of Modern American Fiction."

The information does not need to be in the same order as it appeared in the original article. It can be organized into logical groups and then put in a new order.

▼ Follow this order:

1. As a group, write the marginal notes for the important facts on separate slips of paper. Write only one marginal note on each slip of paper! These papers are now called notes.

2. Place similar notes together in groups.

3. Write a "Heading" or the main idea of each group of notes. See the Outline Model on page 42 if necessary.

4. Number your outline according to the Outline Model.

5. One member of the group will write the finished outline on a transparency or on another piece of paper.

6. Compare your group's outline to another group's outline.

7. Compare your group's outline with the example on page 42.

Step 3: Writing the Summary of Article 1

Now you have your facts organized in logical groups in the form of an outline. You are ready to write a summary paragraph for Article 1.

▼ In your notebook, write your summary in the order of your outline. (Each student in the group will use the group's outline.)

▼ Do not look back at the original article.

Tips for Writing a Summary

▼ Each main point of the outline should be mentioned in the summary.

▼ Use complete sentences.

▼ Use your own words as much as possible.

▼ Write in past tense.

▼ Do not include your own feelings, thoughts, or interpretations in the summary.

When you finish writing the summary, ask yourself these questions to evaluate your own work:

● Did I follow my outline?

● Did I use different words than the article where possible?

PART 3 Comparing Outlines and Summaries

Every outline and summary will be a little different because different groups or people wrote them.

1. Compare your group's outline with another group's outline by answering these questions.

    ● Do the outlines have similar divisions?

    _____

    ● Does each of the subdivisions support the heading?

    _____

2. Compare another group's outline with their summary.

    ● Does the summary follow the order of the outline?

    _____

Here is an example outline and summary of the Stephen Crane Article.

Outline

    I. WRITER (What did he write?)
        A. *Maggie: A Girl of the Streets*—novel, didn't sell
        B. *Red Badge of Courage*—novel, best-seller
        C. Other—short stories
   II. LIFE (What are the basic facts?)
        A. Born 1871, Newark, New Jersey
        B. Family—youngest in family of 14

    C. Two years of college

    D. Went to N.Y. to write

    E. Wife—Cora Taylor

    F. Died from tuberculosis, 1900, at age 29

III. PROFESSION (What did he do to earn a living?)

    A. Newspaper reporter

    B. Reported wars

        1. Spanish-American

        2. Greco-Turkish

IV. TOPICS (What did he write about?)

    A. Wrote about what he saw, realistic

    B. Wrote about how people reacted to real situations

        1. Battle—soldiers

        2. Blizzard

        3. Travels west

        4. Storm, fear

 V. WRITING STYLE

    A. His writing is a balance of reality and imagination

    B. Used irony at the end

VI. IMPORTANCE OF HIS WRITING STYLE

    A. Left a pattern for later writers

    B. Modern American fiction (reality writing) started with Crane

Summary of "Father of Modern American Fiction"

    Stephen Crane was an American writer of novels and short stories. He wrote *Maggie: A Girl of the Streets,* which did not sell well, and *The Red Badge of Courage,* which became a best-seller. He also wrote many other short stories. He was born in 1871 in Newark, New Jersey, the youngest of fourteen children. Because his main interest was writing, after two years of college, he moved to New York to become a writer. His wife was Cora Taylor. He died from tuberculosis in 1900 at age 29. During his short life, he wrote for a newspaper and was later a war correspondent for the Spanish-American and Greco-Turkish wars. He wrote in a realistic style, telling what he and others saw and felt. To get first-hand experience, he went to battles, stayed in a blizzard overnight, traveled in the unsettled West, and experienced fear during a storm at sea. He then wrote about his own and other people's reactions to these situations. Crane's writing was a balance of reality and imagination, and he used irony at the end of his stories. This left a pattern for later writers. The reality writing of modern American fiction started with Stephen Crane, and so he is called the "Father of Modern American Fiction."

PRACTICE 4

Using the Summarizing
Process

Now you will practice the process of summary writing, using Article 2 about Abraham Lincoln.

Step 1: Selecting Main Ideas and Facts

▼ Read Article 2 on pages 46–48.

▼ Underline the most important facts.

▼ Using words or phrases, make marginal notes.

▼ Compare your notes with classmate's work.

Step 2: Organizing the Information

▼ Write the important facts of Article 2 on slips of paper.

▼ Organize those notes by grouping them.

▼ Add headings to your notes.

▼ Write your outline in your notebook.

Step 3: Writing the Summary

▼ Write your summary in your notebook.

Remember:

● The outline organizes the main ideas and facts.

● The summary follows the order of the outline.

Article 2

Now He Belongs to the Ages

Lincoln: An Honored Leader

People of the United States regard Abraham Lincoln as one of the greatest leaders in the history of their country. Every year many thousands of Americans visit the great white marble Lincoln Memorial in Washington, D.C.; they have put his likeness on their money and their stamps; and they have preserved the cabin where some people think he was born as a national shrine.

Lincoln's Story in Brief

Lincoln was born in the year 1809 in the American state of Kentucky. His family were poor farmers. Everyone worked hard just to obtain the necessities of life. Lincoln himself did manual labor on the family farm until he was a young man of twenty-two years. When it was possible, the family sent young Abraham

---

to a local school. During his whole life, however, he had less than one year of formal education. Nevertheless, through natural ability, determination, and study at home, he became one of the most learned men in the world of his time.

Educating himself—with help from a kindly stepmother—was no easy matter. Often young Abraham had to walk many miles to borrow books from others, as his family was too poor to have many books. Because he worked on the family farm during the day, young Abe read and studied mostly at night, lying on the floor and using the fireplace for light.

Hard work had made Lincoln very strong. Often he wrestled in contests with other young men and he always won. He was also known for his great height. By the time he was nineteen years old, he had reached the height of six feet four inches!

But size and strength alone were not the reasons why he became known, respected, and liked by others. He was very gifted in speech. When he was a boy, story-telling was very popular with the people. Young Abraham was a wonderful story-teller, and people would sit quietly for hours to listen to his stories.

Lincoln was also known and respected for many other qualities, such as fairness and honesty. When he became a lawyer, he never asked more for his services than he thought they were worth or more than he thought people could pay. He agreed to defend people in court only when he believed their cases were right and just.

In 1831, at the age of twenty-two, Lincoln left the family farm to make a life of his own. Success did not come quickly or easily. For a short time he was a soldier. Then he ran for political office and lost. Next he tried business and failed so badly that it took him seventeen years to repay his debts.

But Lincoln worked to overcome defeat in politics and failure in business, just as earlier he had studied as a child to overcome lack of schooling. After his unfortunate experience with business, he decided to study law at home. As there were no books where he was then living, he used to walk twenty miles to a town where he could borrow them.

In 1834, not long after he had begun the study of law, Lincoln ran for political office again. This time he was elected to the legislature of the State of Illinois. He was so poor, however, that he had to borrow money from friends to have proper clothes to wear when he went to live in the state capital.

In 1846, Lincoln first ran for national office as a candidate from the State of Illinois for the House of Representatives of the United States Congress. He won the election and served in Congress from 1847–1849. At the end of his term, his party—unhappy with his criticism of a recently ended war between the United States and Mexico—did not renominate him. He returned to Illinois to practice law.

In 1854, Lincoln again won election to the Illinois State Legislature but he shortly resigned to run for the United States Senate. He was unsuccessful. In 1856, he was among those proposed as a candidate for the presidency of the United States. He did not at this time receive the party nomination.

In 1858, Lincoln failed a second time as a candidate to the United States Senate. Even though he failed, however, he became nationally famous and popular because of his position against slavery. In 1860 the Republican Party chose him as its nominee to the United States Presidency. He won the election, and was the first member of the young Republican Party—formed six years earlier in 1854—to become President of the United States.

Lincoln became President of the United States at the moment of the nation's greatest crisis since 1776, when thirteen American colonies declared their independence from Great Britain.

He was a man of goodwill who believed in equality, national unity, and peace. He became President, however, at a time when slavery still existed in some parts of the country; when national unity was threatened because of divided opinion on the question of slavery and other differences between the southern states and the rest of the country; and when the last possibilities to preserve peace were rapidly failing.

Despite the best efforts of Lincoln to preserve peace, war came: Civil War, a war between the States; a war in which fathers fought sons, and brothers fought brothers; a war that caused terrible bloodshed and almost destroyed the nation.

By the end of his presidency, slavery had been ended forever in the nation. Peace had returned. The long, slow work of restoring unity among all the people and of rebuilding the country had begun.

As a leader of a country at war with itself, Lincoln's burdens were very heavy. When peace came on April 9, 1865, a new—and happier—life seemed to have begun for him and for the nation.

But for Lincoln that new and happier life did not last long. On April 14, 1865, he was shot by an assassin while sitting in a Washington, D.C. theater with his wife. The next day he was dead—only six days after the peace.

Lincoln's death brought great sorrow to the country. While millions mourned, a giant funeral ceremony was conducted in Washington, D.C. At the end of the ceremony, his body was sent a third of the way across the continent by train for burial in the State of Illinois. At all hours of the day and night, in all kinds of weather, millions of Americans across the country stood along the railroad tracks, waiting for the funeral train—waiting to pay their last respects to the man who had led them so well, a man who would live forever in their hearts and in the hearts of every new generation of Americans.

When Lincoln died, a former enemy, Edwin M. Stanton, who had later become a friend and member of his cabinet, expressed the profound significance of his death in these few words: "Now he belongs to the ages."

United States Information Agency. Used by permission.

The Summary Report

In many academic subjects you will be expected to summarize one article or to make a combined summary of two or more articles on the same topic. A combined summary is called a summary report. The process is shown in the following diagrams.

A **summary** is a short written statement of all the author's important facts and main ideas (main points).

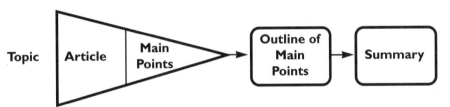

A **summary report** is a short written statement combining the main points (main ideas and facts) of two or more authors.

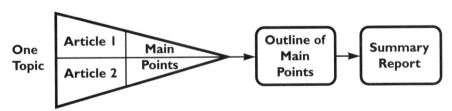

PART I *Summarizing Two or More Articles*

Study the following example of a summary report of two short newspaper articles.

Alcohol-Related Accidents Claim Three Lives

Over the weekend three area youths died in two separate automobile accidents. All three of the dead were students at Cliff High School and were returning from a private canyon party. Thomas Smith, 17, was found dead at the scene of a one-car rollover at 11:55 P.M. Friday, say police.

The other accident was at 12:30 A.M. and involved six area teens. Witnesses reported that the car was traveling west on Canyon Drive at excessive speed and ran into a light pole. The driver, David Johnson, 19, and one passenger, Susan Beck, 16, died on the way to the hospital. The other four were treated for injuries and released. According to one of the survivors, all of the students were returning home from a "beer-bash."

Newville City Council Notes

A committee of mothers from MADD (Mothers Against Drunk Driving) met with the mayor's council to ask for help in stopping the rising number of accidents involving youths and drunk driving.

The mothers reported that alcohol-related arrests and traffic tickets increased about 9 percent over last year.

The mayor assigned a committee to look into this problem and suggest possible solutions at the next council meeting.

Outline

I. Problem—teens and drunk driving

    A. 3 killed after beer party

    B. 9 percent more arrests, traffic tickets

II. Possible solution—mothers ask mayor's council to help

Summary Report

Newville City is having problems with teens and drunk driving. Only this weekend, three teenagers were killed in automobile accidents after a beer party. Also, this year police arrested and gave traffic tickets to nine percent more people who were driving while drunk. Some mothers are worried and asked the mayor's council to help solve this growing community problem.

The Process of Summarizing Two or More Articles

These are the steps for summarizing two or more articles.

1. Read one of the articles.

2. Write marginal notes for important facts.

3. Read the second article.

4. Make marginal notes of additional information not found in the first article.

5. Continue with the remaining articles in this way.

6. Create notes on slips of paper and organize with headings.

7. Write the outline.

8. Write the summary report.

PRACTICE 1

Combining Main Points from Two Articles

▼ Follow the steps above to write a summary report of two articles about Dr. Martin Luther King, Jr.

▼ Write your outline and summary in your notebook.

▼ Attach your notes to the summary.

Dr. Martin Luther King, Jr.: Nobel Prize-Winner

Dr. Martin Luther King, Jr., won the Nobel peace prize in 1964. Dr. King was awarded the peace prize for helping Americans change unfair laws against African-American people. He organized many peaceful mass demonstrations throughout the southern United States and in Washington, D.C. Dr. King developed his ideas through his own experience, as well as through reading books by the American writer Henry David Thoreau and the Russian writer Leo Tolstoy. He especially admired the example of Mahatma Gandhi, who had successfully led a nonviolent revolution to free India of British rule. At 35 years of age, Dr. Martin Luther King, Jr. was the youngest man to ever receive the Nobel peace prize.

Important January Holiday

The United States has a holiday in January named for a great leader, Dr. Martin Luther King, Jr. He was born in Atlanta, Georgia, on January 15, 1929. Georgia and other southern states had been slow to give equal civil rights to African-Americans as well as poor whites, and King wanted a change. When he became a minister in 1954, he began a long road of leadership using nonviolent methods. Many people joined his movement, and in 1963 he led a huge gathering of people to Washington, D.C., to protest unfair government. He said in a talk on that day, "I have a dream that one day this nation will rise up and live out the true meaning of its creed: 'We hold these truths to be self-evident, that all men are created equal.' I have a dream that one day . . . the sons of former slaves and the sons of former slaveholders will be able to sit down together at the table of brotherhood." Because of his efforts, many rights were assured to all races. However, not all people agreed. On April 4, 1968, at age 39, he was killed by an assassin's bullet. Today, Dr. Martin Luther King, Jr.'s birthday is celebrated in honor of his struggle for democracy.

(United States Information Agency. Used by permission.)

PART 2 *Unit Two Assignment Summary Report*

Now you are prepared to begin a summary report on a topic of your choice. For this assignment you will:

▼ Become acquainted with the reference section of your library.

▼ Look for important facts in two different encyclopedia articles about the same topic.

▼ Write notes about the information.

▼ Organize the notes from both articles into one outline.

▼ Write a summary report from the outline.

You will be working on this assignment as you practice the research skills in the rest of this chapter.

I. GETTING STARTED

    A. Be sure you understand the purpose of the assignment.
    B. Your classmates are your audience.
    C. Choose your own topic with the teacher's approval or select one of these topics:

Historical figures	Movie stars	Artists
Frederick Douglass	Gary Cooper	Mary Cassatt
Brigham Young	James Dean	Winslow Homer
Jane Addams	Judy Garland	John Audubon
John F. Kennedy	Clark Gable	Grandma Moses
Ida B. Wells	Grace Kelly	
Clara Barton		

Authors	Musicians	Inventors
Willa Cather	Marian Anderson	Robert Fulton
Emily Dickinson	Dave Brubeck	Henry Ford
Ernest Hemingway	Louis Armstrong	George Washington Carver
John Steinbeck	Ella Fitzgerald	

II. PREWRITING

Prewriting is not necessary because all your information for the summary report will come from the articles you read.

III. CHOOSING INFORMATION   Due:_____

    A. Find the encyclopedias in the library's reference section.

    B. Look up your topic in several encyclopedias.

    C. Choose two articles that seem the most interesting and easiest to read.

    D. Write down the bibliographic information of the encyclopedias here in alphabetical order by the name of encyclopedia. (See pages 54–55.)

Encyclopedia Article 1

_____

_____

Encyclopedia Article 2

_____

_____

    E. Photocopy each article.

    F. Read your articles, underline, and make marginal notes.

    G. Transfer your marginal notes to slips of paper. Remember to put only one piece of information on each piece of paper.

IV. ORGANIZING THE INFORMATION   Due:_____

    A. Organize the notes.

    B. Write the outline.

    C. Have a classmate evaluate your outline. Make changes if necessary.

V. WRITE YOUR SUMMARY REPORT   Due:_____

    A. Look only at your outline while you write or type the Summary Report.

    B. Write or type a reference list. Remember to put your sources in alphabetical order.

    C. Write or type a title page. Follow the model.

VI. REVISE YOUR SUMMARY REPORT   Due:_____

    A. Have a classmate evaluate your paper and make revision suggestions.

    B. Write your paper again, making the corrections necessary.

VII. EDIT YOUR SUMMARY REPORT   Due:_____

    A. Have your teacher or a native English speaker indicate spelling, punctuation, and grammar errors.

    B. Read your report aloud.

    C. Make the corrections and rewrite your summary the final time.

Preparing the Folder to Turn In: Due:_____

▼ Put your completed summary report in a three-hole pocket folder. Make sure that the pages are in this order:

Title page
Outline page
Summary report—one typed or two written (double-spaced) pages
Reference list

▼ Place these items in the pockets of the folder:

Note papers from notes for two encyclopedia articles paperclipped or in a small letter-type envelope
Photocopies of the two encyclopedia articles you used
First draft of the paper

PART 3 *Listing References*

With this assignment you are beginning to do library research and your research sources are encyclopedias. This is because encyclopedias are easy to find in a library and they are easy to read and use. Later, as your skills in library research improve, you will seldom use encyclopedias except to get some general information, key words, or to give you other clues to aid you in more advanced library research. Encyclopedias are not generally listed as references in academic papers.

In doing library research, it is important to list where you got any information you used from any source. This information, also called bibliographic information, is put in your paper in a very specific way. All the styles (APA, MLA, Turabian, etc.) are exacting. In other words, you must follow the form exactly. In APA style, all sources are listed on a separate page entitled "References." (For a model of how to set up a reference page in APA style, see p. 25.) The following example shows how to list encyclopedias on a reference page in APA style.

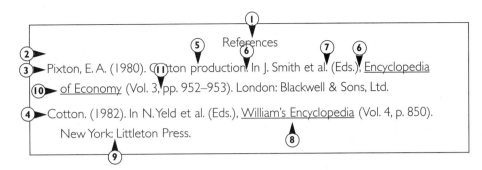

1. Title—References.

2. Make three line spaces between the title and the first source.

3. Put each reference in alphabetical order by last name of author.

4. If there is no author, write the title of the article first.

5. Write the title of the article with only the first word capitalized. The title is not underlined or put in quotation marks.

6. Use a comma or a period to separate each piece of information. Be careful to notice where a period is used and where a comma is used.

7. Write only the name of the first editor and put "et al." after it when there are more than four editors. Shorten the word *Editor* to *Ed.* and put it in parentheses. If there is more than one editor, use *Eds.*

8. The title of the encyclopedia is underlined.

9. Put the location where the book is published, a colon, and then the book publisher last.

10. Indent all lines after the first line of each source.

11. Put some information in parentheses such as the year, volume, page numbers, and editor.

Answer these questions:

▼ What is the order of the information in each entry?

_____

_____

▼ How many spaces are between the lines?

_____

▼ In what order are the entries?

_____

▼ How is more than one page indicated?

_____

PART 4 *The Title Page*

Another requirement for this assignment is to have a title page. The title page of a research paper is the first page. There are two types: the traditional style and the APA style.

A traditional title page gives:

- the title of the paper
- the author's name
- the class for which the paper was written
- the name of the teacher
- the date the final draft of the paper was written

An APA title page gives:

- the title of the paper
- the author's name
- the author's university

The following pages give instructions for typing both types of title pages on a word processor. For many courses the traditional title page is used. Check with your teacher to see which title page is best for each research paper.

Traditional Title Page

(Center the cursor and press ENTER 12 times)

Title of Paper
(Press ENTER 11 times)

Student's Name
(Press ENTER 11 times)

Class Name
(Press Enter 2 times)
Instructor's Name
(Press Enter 2 times)
Month, Day, Year

APA Title Page

The first few words of the title
(press ENTER 2 times)
Page number 1
(press ENTER 12 times)

Complete Title of Paper
(Press ENTER 2 times)
Student's Name
(Press ENTER 2 times)
Name of University

PART 5 *Summary Report Evaluations*

The success of the final written paper is based on the correctness of each step in the process. Therefore, as you work through this first library assignment, each step needs to be evaluated by you or a classmate and your teacher. Here are some questions to guide the evaluations of each step:

Evaluation of your notes

- Did you put only one piece of information on each paper?
- Are your notes in your own words (paraphrased)?

Evaluation of your outline

- Do the major divisions (I, II, III) show the organization of the information?
- Do the subdivisions (A, B, C) support each major division?
- Does the outline use words and phrases?
- Are the correct numbers and letters used?

First draft

After the evaluations of your notes and outline are completed, write the first draft of your summary report in your notebook. A first draft is the first time you write from your outline.

You often learn more about the strengths and weaknesses of your own paper by evaluating the paper of a classmate. The following is a peer evaluation sheet for the first draft of the summary report. Use it to evaluate another classmate's paper.

Peer evaluation of the summary report—first draft

▼ Compare each point of the paper with the models for title page, outline, paper, and reference page.

▼ Put *S* (Satisfactory) and *U* (Unsatisfactory) in the blanks.

▼ Put the total number of *S*'s and *U*'s at the top.

Name of Writer _____   Total Satisfactory_____
Name of Evaluator _____   Total Unsatisfactory ____
Date_____

Title Page
_____   1. Title page is in the correct form.
Outline
_____   2. Has the title outline.
_____   3. Is in the correct form (I, II, A, B, l, 2).
_____   4. Punctuation is correct.
_____   5. Headings after Roman numerals (I, II, etc.) are major divisions of the topic.
_____   6. Subdivisions (A, B, etc.) support the major division.
_____   7. Is in words and phrases (not sentences).
_____   8. Is in the student's own words (not copied).
Paper
_____   9. Is one page typed or two pages handwritten.
_____   10. Has margins on all four sides.
_____   11. Is written on only one side of each page.
_____   12. Is typed in normal-size type or neatly written.
_____   13. Is double-spaced.
_____   14. First word of each paragraph is indented one-half inch.
_____   15. Matches the outline.
Reference List
_____   16. Reference page exists.
_____   17. Has a title.
_____   18. Has at least two references in alphabetical order.
_____   19. References follow APA style.

Optional for first draft

_____20. Three-hole pocket folder exists with the student's name on the cover.

_____21. Pages in the three-hole folder are in this order: title page, outline, paper, reference list.

_____22. Copies of two encyclopedia articles are in the folder.

_____23. Notes from two encyclopedia articles are in the folder.

Tell the writer what you liked about the paper. Did you learn anything new as you read it?

_____

_____

_____

_____

Write any additional suggestions to improve this paper.

_____

_____

_____

_____

Second and Final Drafts

After looking carefully at your classmate's evaluation and suggestions, write the second draft of the summary report, making necessary revisions. Have a classmate or the teacher look over your second draft and point out any grammar, punctuation, or spelling errors that need attention. Make the necessary corrections and write your final draft.

Expanding Academic Writing Skills

In this unit, you will learn to expand your academic writing skills from a well-formed paragraph, to an essay, to a research paper. The important features of these three types of writing are shown on the next page. Also on the next page you will find a list of questions that you will know how to answer by the end of this unit.

In this unit you will:

▼ Study the relationship between reading and writing

▼ Develop and narrow a research question

▼ Write a cause-and-effect research paper

You will also learn to:

▼ Write a planning outline and a final outline

▼ Write a formal introduction

▼ Write a formal conclusion

Other skills you will practice are:

▼ Adding transitions

▼ Putting a research paper together

Here is a brief comparison of a paragraph, an essay, and a research paper written in expository form. As you compare the three, notice how the main parts of each are related.

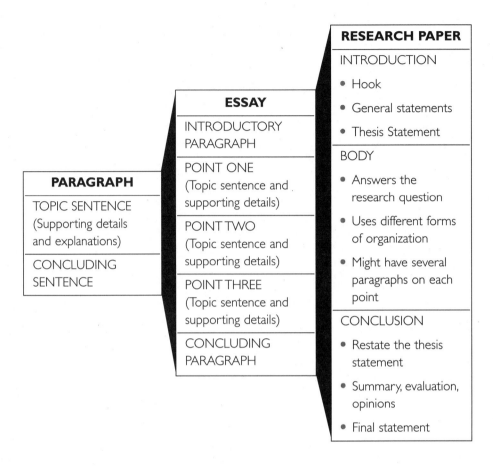

PARAGRAPH

TOPIC SENTENCE
(Supporting details and explanations)

CONCLUDING SENTENCE

ESSAY

INTRODUCTORY PARAGRAPH

POINT ONE
(Topic sentence and supporting details)

POINT TWO
(Topic sentence and supporting details)

POINT THREE
(Topic sentence and supporting details)

CONCLUDING PARAGRAPH

RESEARCH PAPER

INTRODUCTION

- Hook
- General statements
- Thesis Statement

BODY

- Answers the research question
- Uses different forms of organization
- Might have several paragraphs on each point

CONCLUSION

- Restate the thesis statement
- Summary, evaluation, opinions
- Final statement

Read these questions. By the time you finish this unit, you should know the answers to all of them. How many can you answer now?

1. Relationship of reading to writing

   - What do reading and writing have in common?
   - What is the purpose of an abstract?
   - How do you choose the most important points in an article or book?

2. Types of writing

   - How are a paragraph, an essay, and a report similar? How are they different?
   - What is the difference between a summary report and a research paper?
   - What is the reason for a research question?
   - What is the difference between a research question and a thesis statement?
   - What is a research paper?
   - What does "narrowing the topic" mean?

3. Outlines

   - What is an outline?
   - What is the outline form?
   - What is the purpose of a planning outline?
   - What is the purpose of a final outline?

4. Formal introduction

   - Can you find the three parts easily?
   - Can you write a good introduction?

5. Formal conclusion

   - Can you find the three parts easily?
   - Can you write a good conclusion?

6. Transitions

   - Do you know how to use transitions?
   - What do transitions do?
   - How many transitions are used in each paragraph?
   - What is the correct punctuation?

7. Putting it together

   - Do you know how to go from a topic to a research question to a thesis statement to a planning outline?
   - Do you know what parts go into your final paper?

The Relationship Between Reading and Writing

Writers write their ideas and thoughts for someone to read. Readers, in turn, hope the ideas and thoughts will be easy to understand as they read. Therefore, both the reader and the writer are working with the words on paper.

Words can be organized in many different ways, but academic papers in English have specific ways that ideas and thoughts are organized. Here are some points to consider.

PART 1 *Reading and Writing*

1. When you read for academic purposes, you look for the main ideas, the most important points, and the things you want or need to remember. Reading can be illustrated this way:

2. When you write for academic purposes, such as a report or an essay, you start with a main idea, determine the sub-points of the main idea or topic, then expand these sub-points with examples, facts, descriptions, details, and/or experiences that explain or support the main idea. Writing can be illustrated this way:

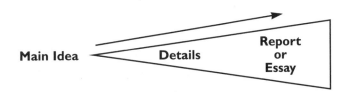

3. When you write in a college setting, you want the reader (usually the professor or a classmate) to understand your main point or points. I you have provided enough explanations in the form of descriptions, examples, facts, and experiences, the reader will understand and remember at least the main idea. This relationship can be illustrated this way:

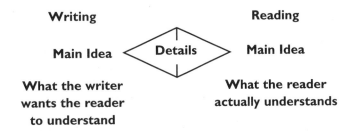

4. If you do not include enough details, facts, examples, descriptions, and/or experiences, the reader will not understand, and the communication between writer and reader is incomplete. The relationship looks like this:

This is why it is important in academic writing to make a clear statement of your main idea and carefully select those details that will best support your idea. Starting with a main idea and using enough good details will help you communicate with the reader.

PART 2 *The Abstract*

Another important element of an academic paper for the reader and the writer is the abstract. Abstracts are found

- at the beginning of many academic papers
- in library indexes on computers or in special books

You can see an abstract in Unit One at the beginning of the research paper on page 19. You will learn how to write an abstract for your own papers in Chapter 20.

To help you discover for yourself what an abstract is, complete the following activities:

▼ In five minutes, tell a classmate about a movie you saw recently.

▼ In one minute, tell your classmate about the same movie.

▼ Consider this question: What did you have to do in order to tell about the movie in one minute?

▼ In a paragraph, write down what you did during the busiest four hours of your day.

▼ In one sentence, do the same.

▼ Consider this question: How was the second writing different from the first?

The five-minute movie activity and the five-minute writing activity are like a summary.

The one-minute narration and the one-minute sentence are similar to an abstract.

Have you discovered for yourself what an abstract is? Write your own definition of an abstract. Compare it with a classmate's.

_____

_____

Here is a *summary* of the Stephen Crane article from Chapter 5.

Summary of "Father of Modern American Fiction"

Stephen Crane was an American writer of novels and short stories. His most famous novel was the best-selling *The Red Badge of Courage*. Born in 1871, the youngest of 14 children, he was first interested in becoming a professional baseball player. After two years of college, he moved to New York to become a writer. He married Cora Taylor. He died of tuberculosis at the age of 29. For most of his life, he was a newspaper writer or correspondent. He wrote about what he saw and about how people reacted to real situations, such as battles and storms. Crane's writing was important because he wrote with a balance of reality and imagination, and he used irony at the end of his stories. This left a pattern for later writers. The reality writing of modern American fiction started with Stephen Crane, and so he is called the "Father of Modern American Fiction."

This is an *abstract* of the same article.

Stephen Crane (1871–1900), was a writer of novels and short stories. He wrote about how people reacted to real situations and ended his stories with irony. This technique was copied by later American writers, so he is called the father of modern American fiction.

Here is a definition of an abstract. Does this definition match your definition in any way?

> An abstract is a short paragraph that gives the most important main ideas of the article.

P R A C T I C E 1

Writing an Abstract

Write an abstract by using the principles you have discovered and learned. In the space below, write an abstract about the Abraham Lincoln article on page 46.

P A R T 3 *Using an Abstract*

Because you will probably not have time to read entire articles to decide if there is information you need, you can use the abstract of the article to find out the most important main points in advance. Since abstracts are used at the beginning of a lot of professional writing, how can abstracts help you in doing library research?

P R A C T I C E 2

Using Abstracts

▼ Imagine that you are getting married and want to find information on inexpensive weddings.

▼ The following abstracts are about weddings. Look at each abstract and guess what specific information in the article would be helpful.

▼ Write your guesses on a piece of paper.

▼ Compare your answers with your classmate's.

Abstract 1

Christensen, A. (1995, June). Wedding rings 'out of sight.' <u>Love and Marriage</u>, 13, 15–16.

Prices for wedding rings are increasing because of the growing fashion of purchasing diamond rings for both men and women. Therefore, some couples are looking for alternatives. The author explains several other ways to show marriage vows, such as special gifts or other less expensive stones.

Guess:

_____

_____

Abstract 2

Beckstead, L. (1995, Winter). Honeymoons: Finding a sweet delight. Travel, Travel, Travel, 43–61.

This is an extensive list of honeymoon vacation packages offered at various famous vacation hotels including prices for rooms, meals, drinks, entertainment, etc.

Guess:

_____

_____

Abstract 3

Howell, D. (1994, April 6). Jazzy weddings. News about Town, B9.

Modern weddings can be held in a variety of locations besides churches—in fact, anywhere you can get a member of the clergy to go. The author describes the most unlikely places weddings occur, such as on bicycles or while skydiving.

Guess:

_____

_____

Preparing for a Cause-and-Effect Research Paper

INTRODUCTION

In Unit Two you learned to write a summary report. In this unit you will learn to write a research paper. How are these two library papers similar? How are they different?

A summary report is a short written report of the main ideas and important facts of two or more articles.

The summary report does not include any additional information you might know because you are only reporting the ideas or facts written by other authors.

A research paper is a combination of facts and ideas from several sources that answer a research question.

A research paper does not use all the information you find on a topic. It uses only those facts and ideas that answer the research question. Thus, your research task is to find sources, such as books, articles, or parts of articles that will help you answer the research question you ask.

PART 1   *Developing a Research Question*

A research question is a question you will answer in your research paper. It guides your search for information. Different questions will guide the researcher to different information.

Step 1: Asking questions about the topic

To create a research question, you must first ask yourself important questions about your topic. Since the research paper for this unit will be about cause and effect, your research question will include one of these words:

cause = to make something happen

effect = the result or consequence

Here are some possible research questions on the causes and effects of divorce:

1. What are the causes of divorce?
2. What are the main causes of divorce in Mexico?
3. What are the two major causes of divorce in the United States?
4. What are the effects of divorce?
5. What are the effects of divorce on men?
6. What are the effects of divorce on women?
7. What are the effects of divorce on children?
8. What are the effects of divorce in my country?

Many of the questions above are too general for the three-page paper required in this unit. A general research question is useful, however, to begin thinking about the topic and discover a more specific or narrowed question.

Step 2: Prewriting with a general research question

Once you choose a general research question, the next step is to write down ideas that come to your mind when you think about the general question. This is a brainstorming method called listing. Listing is an effective way to begin writing many papers.

PRACTICE 1

Prewriting by Listing

DIRECTIONS: Choose one general question from the list above about divorce and write down some ideas you might want to discuss in a research paper. Write the general question and several important ideas about it.

General question:

_____

_____

List important ideas about the question.

_____

_____

_____

Step 3: Narrowing the topic

You may have to make a number of lists before you develop a research question that is narrow enough for a three-page paper. Some cause-and-effect topics are so large that in order to narrow the topic, you might want to look only at the causes or only at the effects, whichever interests you the most.

Each research question guides the writer to look for specific information that will answer the question. The answers to one question may need different ideas, examples, and facts than the answer to another question. As a result, the research question you choose limits your paper to only part of the topic. This is how you begin to narrow your topic.

For example, if you choose a question that asks about the causes of divorce, the paper will only be about causes, such as:

- disagreements about money
- immaturity
- cultural differences between husband and wife

Even though it may be interesting, you will not include information like this:

- the effects of divorce on children
- the differences in the divorce laws of different countries
- the cost of divorce
- the reasons divorce is accepted in one culture and not another

These ideas should not be included because they do not directly relate to the research question on the cause of divorce.

Step 4: Narrowing a research question during your research

You can change the research question at any time during the process of preparing your paper. If you started with the general research question, "What are the causes of divorce?" you already may have listed some causes and changed the research question to "How do money problems and different interests cause divorce?" but you don't know what you will find as you do research.

As you begin looking for information in the library, you might find a very interesting article on the problems couples have with money, which will answer part of the question. Another article says more divorces occur when people marry very young, or marry people of another culture and gives many interesting facts and examples. These are good ideas and you have already found a source for information. So you change your research question to read,

"How do conflicts about money, immaturity, and cultural differences cause divorce?"

This is a much more specific research question, which will now guide you to find more information on these three points.

Here is an example of a narrowed research question that one student made on the effects of blindness:

> **"What are some specific details, examples, and statistics that show how becoming blind as an adult causes depression, divorce, and a change of occupation?"**

Notice that it is very specific and it will guide the writer to search for more supporting details.

Step 5: Using a cause-and-effect chart to narrow your topic

Many people start with a long list of ideas about a topic and then narrow it down. A list of causes and effects, however, can become confusing. This is because any given cause can also be seen as an effect in another situation. For example, if a poor country tries to conquer a rich neighboring country, poverty can be seen as a cause of war. However, if war destroys people's homes and farms, the resulting poverty can be seen as an effect of war.

The following diagram shows how causes can also be seen as effects.

After you use a chart like this to generate ideas, you will have to choose which of the many causes and effects to write about. Some of the effects may be more interesting to you than others, and information on some may not be available in the library. As you choose what to include, you will also have to take into consideration how long the paper is supposed to be. All of these considerations help you to narrow the topic to the appropriate length.

Step 6: Using a research question to reduce your reading time

Not every article or book on your topic will answer your research question. You will need to choose only those articles and books that are directly related to the research question. Here are some ideas to help you:

- Read the abstract of the most important ideas in the article to see if they answer your research question.

- Look through the table of contents to find chapters or parts of chapters that may answer your research question.

- If the reading has no abstract or table of contents, quickly read the introduction and the conclusion as well as the main ideas at the beginning of each paragraph.

- When you find information that will help you answer your research question, slow down your reading speed and look more closely.

- Carefully read the section that answers your research question, photocopy it, underline and take notes on the important facts and ideas.

Remember, you will not need to read those articles or parts of articles that do not answer your research question. So the research question can help you limit your reading to the important areas for your research paper.

PART 2 *Unit 3 Assignment: Cause-and-Effect Research Paper*

Now you are prepared to begin a research paper on a cause-and-effect topic of your choice. You will be practicing these new skills:

▼ Narrowing a cause-and-effect topic

▼ Using periodicals in your research

▼ Writing an introduction and a conclusion

The next four chapters will take you step by step through the new research and writing skills. However, you are ready to get started on this paper.

I. GETTING STARTED

A. Choose a topic you are interested in, with the teacher's approval, or select one of these topics:

avalanches	blindness	hurricanes	floods
deafness	earthquakes	erosion	famine
volcanoes	fires	pollution	tornadoes

B. Create a research question about your topic.
For example: "What are the main causes and effects of . . . ?"
"What are the causes of . . . ?"
"What are the effects of . . . ?"

II. PREWRITING   Due:_____

A. Brainstorm about possible ideas to use with the research question.

B. Choose ideas that interest you most.

Due:_____

III. CHOOSING INFORMATION ON YOUR TOPIC   Due:_____

Repeat these steps, if necessary, until you have enough details for your report. You must use at least two library sources.

A. Find an encyclopedia article.
1. Write down the bibliographic information for the encyclopedia.

2. Make a photocopy of the article at the library.

B. Find a periodical article (professional journal, magazine, newspaper) by looking in the *Reader's Guide to Periodical Literature.*

1. Ask the librarian to show you the location of the *Reader's Guide to Periodical Literature* and ask how to use it to find the most useful article.

2. Write down the bibliographic information for the periodical article. (See Chapter 12, p. 102.)

3. Photocopy the article.

C. Read for information.

1. Underline and/or make marginal notes of information that helps you answer your research question.

D. Narrow the research question.

1. As you find information, make a more specific research question.

2. If you don't find enough information, change the research question.

E. Narrow the topic to the length of your paper. Choose the information that will best fit the length of your paper.

F. Make note papers. Write only one note on each paper.

IV. ORGANIZING THE INFORMATION   Due:_____

A. Put the note papers in logical groups and put headings on the groups.

B. Make a planning outline of the information.

C. Create the thesis statement from the ideas in the research question.

V. WRITING YOUR FIRST DRAFT   Due:_____

A. Follow your planning outline to write your paper.

B. Write a formal introduction with a thesis statement.

C. Write a formal conclusion.

D. Organize each paragraph with a main idea and supporting details.

E. Use transitions in the paper.

F. Write a title page and a reference page of your bibliography.

G. Write a final outline.

VI. REVISING AND REWRITING   Due:_____
(SECOND DRAFT OR MORE)

A. Have a classmate evaluate your paper.

B. Turn it in to the teacher for an evaluation also.

C. Reorganize the paper so that it is more logical, and has better sentences, well-organized paragraphs, etc.

D. Change the final outline to match the paper.

VII. EDIT AND REWRITING (FINAL DRAFT)   Due:_____

A. Read your paper aloud.

B. Correct spelling, punctuation, and grammar errors.

Preparing the folder to turn in:

1. Put your completed research paper in a three-hole pocket folder. Make sure that the pages are in this order:
    - Title page
    - Final outline
    - Research paper
    - Reference list

2. Place these items in the pockets of the folder:
    - Planning outline
    - Photocopies
    - Note papers
    - First drafts of paper

P A R T 3 *Planning Your Research Time*

The following chart illustrates the amount of time you will probably use on each step of the process of writing a research paper. Which step will take the least time? Which will take the most time? Why? How much time will you actually use in writing the paper?

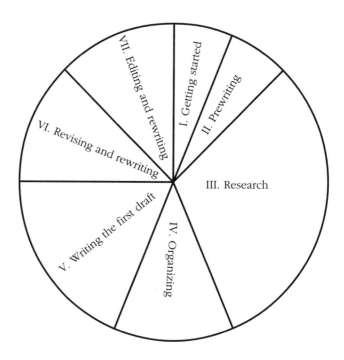

Writing an Introduction

Introductions are everywhere. Whenever you meet new people, the first thing you do is introduce yourself and ask their names. Then you may find out a little more about them, such as where they are from, why they are here, or some common likes and dislikes. Sometimes after an introduction, you will decide if you want to get to know a person better.

An introductory paragraph at the beginning of an academic paper has the same purpose. It introduces the topic to the readers.

PART 1 *The Introduction*

The introduction begins the paper. It has three parts:

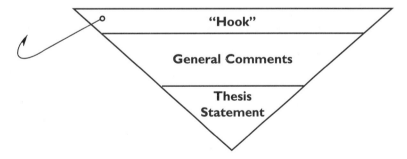

1. A **"hook"** is usually the first sentence. It is an interesting or emotional comment about the topic. It is used to catch the reader's attention and interest.

2. **General comments** include several sentences that give interesting background information about the topic.

3. The **thesis statement** is the last sentence in the introduction. It is the most important sentence in the introduction. It states the specific topic of the essay.

Example:

The following paragraph is the introductory paragraph of a paper.

The "hook" is <u>underlined</u>.

The general comments are in normal type.

The thesis statement is **bold.**

> <u>In the early history of the United States, it was believed that people out of work or unemployed were lazy and simply did not want to work.</u> They were often treated badly or punished for their laziness and lack of responsibility. Today, however, people look at the unemployed differently because unemployment is often caused by outside problems. **Some of the causes of unemployment are problems of high inflation, seasonal jobs, and changes in government laws.**

The topic of this paper is the causes for unemployment.

The second paragraph will talk about high inflation.

The third paragraph will talk about seasonal jobs.

The fourth paragraph will talk about changes in government laws.

The last paragraph will be the conclusion.

PRACTICE 1

Identifying Parts of an Introduction

▼ Read each introductory paragraph.

▼ Underline the hook.

▼ Circle the thesis statement and read it carefully.

▼ Guess what parts of the topic will be discussed in the paper.

Introduction 1

> **Jogging**
>
> He is quiet. His heart beats quickly as he perspires profusely from his adventure. His body has experienced the fun of play and the challenge of work. He has just discovered the benefits of jogging, the quickest and most efficient way for most people to achieve physical fitness.
>
> Guess:
>
> _____
>
> _____

Introduction 2

Youth Suicide

In ancient times, suicide was a heroic way of ending a life. In Japan, a person suffering a "loss of face" committed hara-kiri. In Greece, to save his honor, a warrior fell on his sword. Today, committing suicide is not so heroic. It is considered a major social problem because it is the third largest cause of death among students. What causes young adults to commit suicide and what is the effect on their peers?

Guess:

_____

_____

Introduction 3

New Solutions to Old Problems

Just about everybody has heard of the population explosion. Many experts tell us that the world will soon come to an end if we don't control the birth rate. Demographers say that there will be too many people. Economists say that there aren't enough resources. Agriculturalists say that there will be too little food. Even though most experts want to limit the number of people on earth, they do not seriously consider human creativity. In recent years, this world crisis has caused innovative scientists to discover new concepts of using space, develop new types of industries, and create more productive varieties of seeds and fertilizers.

Guess:

_____

_____

PART 2 *The Thesis Statement*

The thesis statement is usually written at the end of the introduction. The purpose of the thesis statement is to:

- give the specific topic of the paper
- point to the topic parts that will be discussed in the rest of the paper
  (Note: A title is NOT the thesis statement)

In the introductory paragraph about jogging, the thesis statement is:

"He has just discovered the benefits of jogging, the quickest and most efficient way for most people to achieve physical fitness."

The specific topic of the paper is "jogging."
The topic parts that will be discussed are:
Jogging is a quick way to fitness.
Jogging is efficient.

PRACTICE 2

Identifying the Parts of a Thesis Statement

Work with a partner and follow the steps below for writing a thesis statement.

Step 1:

▼ Identify the specific topic and topic parts of these thesis statements about the effect of teenagers on shopping malls.

▼ Underline the topic and circle the topic parts of each thesis statement.

Thesis statements:

1. Since a lot of customers at a mall are teenagers, the clothing stores have the latest teen styles and fads.

2. Because teenagers love malls, the restaurants at malls all offer food that teenagers like.

3. Worried parents try to help their teenagers find more productive activities, such as sports, music lessons, and clubs.

4. Thus, businesspeople decorate and design malls to please their teenage customers.

Step 2:

▼ Read the introduction.

▼ Choose one of the thesis statements above.

▼ Write your chosen thesis statement at the end of the introduction.

Introductory paragraph without a thesis statement:

Malls couldn't exist without teenagers! They flood the malls every weekend to visit with their friends. They also shop, eat, buy music, play arcade games, and go to the movies. In fact, today's teenagers spend more time and money at malls than any previous generation has.

_____

_____

_____

_____

Step 3:

▼ Determine the major divisions that will be in your paper, using the specific parts of the thesis statement that you wrote above.

▼ Use your imagination.

▼ What parts of the topic might be discussed in the paper?

▼ Write these parts as headings in the outline below. (Note: Not every paper topic needs four parts.)

   I. Introduction

  II. _____

 III. _____

 IV. _____

  V. _____

 VI. Conclusion

Step 4:

▼ Compare your outline with a classmate's outline.

▼ Discuss the ways in which your outline is different from your classmate's outline.

▼ Talk about how the thesis statements determine the direction, or major divisions, of the paper.

PART 3   *Writing a Thesis Statement*

The thesis statement is created by using the ideas in the research question. One way to write a thesis statement is to turn the research question into a sentence, rather than a question. Another way is to create a new sentence. In either case, a good thesis statement always includes the topic. In addition, it can point the reader to the main ideas you are going to include in your paper.

Sample research question:

How do conflicts about money, immaturity, and cultural differences cause divorce?

Sample thesis statement:

Divorce is caused by immaturity, cultural differences, and conflicts about money.

Thesis statements can be very specific or quite general. A general thesis statement states the topic but does not list the topic parts that will be discussed in the body of the paper. The following thesis statements are general.

"There are three main reasons for divorce in the 20th century."

"Hurricanes cause a vast amount of damage."

"Several physiological problems can cause deafness."

Long research papers often use general thesis statements. However, because you will write short research papers in this course, you will use specific thesis statements.

A specific thesis statement not only gives the topic of the paper, but also tells the parts that will be in the paper. The more specific the thesis statement, the more the reader can tell in advance what will be in your paper. The thesis statement below is specific. Notice the topic and the parts that will be in the paper.

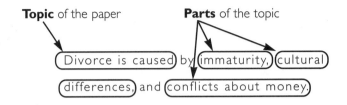

This specific thesis statement could be put in your planning outline like this:

Topic: Causes of divorce

Major divisions in the outline

    I. Introduction

   II. Immaturity

 III. Cultural differences

 IV. Conflicts about money

  V. Conclusion

PRACTICE 3

Identifying the Topic and the Major Divisions of the Outline

▼ Read this research question.

> What are some specific details, examples, and statistics that show how becoming blind as an adult causes depression, divorce, and a change of occupation?

Here is a specific thesis statement made from that question.

> ### Becoming blind as an adult frequently causes depression, divorce, and a change of occupation.

By looking carefully at this thesis statement, can you find the topic and the major divisions of the outline that will be discussed in the paper?

Topic: *Effects of Blindness on Adults*

Major Divisions of the Outline:

    I. Introduction

   II. *Depression*

 III. *Divorce*

 IV. *Change of Occupation*

  V. Conclusion

PRACTICE 4

Finding the Topic and Major Divisions of the Outline

▼ Read each introduction.

▼ Underline the hook.

▼ Write the general topic of the paper and the major divisions in the outline.

Introduction 1

Native Americans

    Native Americans have lived on the American continent for thousands of years. As their numbers grew, they divided into tribes and settled different parts of the country. When they did this, their lifestyles also became different from each other. Some lived in the mountains, while others lived on the prairies. Some tribes lived in tepees. Others lived in caves or in homes built out of mud or sticks. Two tribes in particular, the Navajo and the Cheyenne, were very different. They differed in both their histories and their lifestyles.

The topic of this paper is

_____

The major divisions are:

    I. Introduction

   II. _____

  III. _____

  IV. Conclusion

Introduction 2

Flying

    While watching birds easily fly through the air, people wondered if they could do the same thing. Some tried. They tied feathers to their arms and legs and jumped off cliffs; they strapped on wings made of paper and jumped from buildings. Finally, after many years of experimenting with balloons, wings on wheels, and gliders, the Wright brothers, in 1903, attached a motor and two propellers to a two-winged glider and flew! The successful flight of the Wright brothers caused the eventual development of private planes, air-passenger carriers, and, most recently, space exploration.

The topic of this paper is

_____

The major divisions are:

   I. Introduction

  II. _____

 III. _____

 IV. Conclusion

Introduction 3

Snow

    The earth is silent after the night's snowstorm. All is quiet. All is white. The snow has changed the ground from green, beige, and brown to white and black. Snow hangs from the bare trees like white beards. Slowly, the world wakes up. The snowplow roars down the street, clearing the snow and spreading salt. The bus arrives to pick up the waiting children. The streets fill up with people in cars going to work. The temperature turns cold, below freezing, and the streets become like glass. Some people never get to work because they slide off the road or bump into other cars while trying to stop. Snow is the cause of both good and bad events in our lives.

The topic of this paper is

_____

The major divisions are:

   I. Introduction

  II. _____

 III. _____

 IV. Conclusion

PRACTICE 5

Writing a Specific Thesis Statement and the Major Divisions of an Outline

Change this research question on education into a specific thesis statement.

"What are the effects of education on my life?"

Follow these steps:

▼ Brainstorm to create a narrower research question.

▼ Change the narrowed research question into a specific thesis statement.

▼ Write a possible outline showing only the major divisions.

P R A C T I C E 6

Writing an Introduction

Write an introduction for the topic in Practice 5. Follow these steps:

▼ Begin with a hook.

▼ Add general information, description, or background information.

▼ Write the specific thesis statement from Practice 5 at the end of the introduction.

> **Now you are ready to write the introduction
> to the research paper for this unit.**

Writing a Conclusion

CHAPTER 10

INTRODUCTION

The conclusion of a paper can be compared to saying good-bye. Often when you leave someone, you mention some important parts of your visit. You might say, "Don't forget to call me and tell me about . . . ", or "I enjoyed hearing about . . . " When you are at the end of your conversation, you probably close it in a comfortable way for everyone.

A conclusion in an academic paper has a similar purpose. It is the way to tell the reader that you have finished discussing the topic.

PART 1 *The Conclusion*

The conclusion ends the paper. It tells the reader that you have finished your essay. It has three parts:

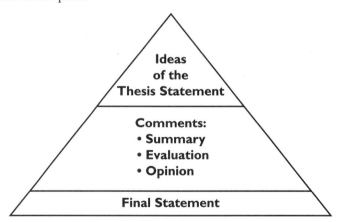

1. The ideas of the thesis statement appear in the first sentence of the conclusion. They are in different words than those in the introduction.

2. Comments can include a summary of all the main ideas, an evaluation of the ideas, and/or the writer's opinion.

3. The final statement is a final thought that "ties up" the topic for the reader.

With your classmates, identify the three parts of a conclusion in these examples.

Conclusion 1

The Effects of Volcanoes

Volcanoes seem to have a significant effect on the climate and the soils in the areas in which they occur. The climates seem to become cooler over a long period of time after an eruption, and the soils become enriched as the volcanic lava and ash are broken down. Therefore, volcanoes are both destructive and beneficial to nature.

Conclusion 2

The Causes of Laughter

To summarize, people laugh a good portion of their lives for various reasons. Babies laugh when something no longer is frightening to them. Adults sometimes laugh when they are trying to cover up a fear, or when they remember something in the past that at the time was frustrating, or when a behavior seems inconsistent with the situation. Laughter helps people go through hard times in life and helps them enjoy situations. It is, therefore, important that society never forget how to laugh.

PRACTICE 1

Identifying the Three Parts in a Conclusion

▼ Read each research question and the conclusion.

▼ Underline the possible thesis statement ideas.

▼ In the margin, write the type of comment used: summary, evaluation, and/or opinion.

▼ Star (*) the beginning of the "tie" or final statement.

Conclusion 1

(Research Question: "What are the effects of running?")

Run for Your Life

In summary, exercise is the way to be healthier and to live longer, and running is a great example of such exercise. Among many other benefits, running keeps calcium in the bones to protect them against osteoporosis; helps reduce the risk of heart disease; reduces problems associated with excess weight such as diabetes, gall bladder disease, gout, and certain cancers; helps muscles increase flexibility and improve strength; helps relieve stress; and even makes people become more intelligent, live longer, and feel more joy. For these, and many other reasons, people should run as a habitual activity. In essence, running means to be young forever!

(Alfredo Garnica—Mexico)

Conclusion 2:

(Research Question: "What is the real cost of nuclear energy?")

The Accelerating Cost of Nuclear Energy

In conclusion, the power produced by nuclear plants is neither cheap, safe, nor clean. Even though scientists can estimate the price of producing nuclear energy, they cannot predict the price that people will have to pay for living in a world full of radiation. After a few very dangerous explosions, many things have to be reevaluated. One of the people who lived close to Three Mile Island during the accident in 1979 said, "Even if only a little bit of radiation escapes from a nuclear facility, causing cancer in you or your child, you will not be comforted by the fact that it was just a little bit." There is no such thing as a one-hundred-percent safe nuclear energy plant, and there is no way to calculate the price of the life of a human being.

(Iwona Bednarczyk—Poland)

Conclusion 3:

(Research Question: "What are the reasons to avoid abortion?")

Your Choice, but Not Your Life

The fight against abortion will continue in the world and people will continue to look for a real, precise, and scientific answer to the question of when life begins. Meanwhile, as we find answers, we should give the benefit of the doubt to life. For example, if we are driving a car in the night and we see a dark shadow that looks like a person, should we run through it just because we are not sure the shadow is a human being? In the same way, we should not let abortion take the lives of children just because we are not sure they are yet living human beings.

(Rafael Delgado—Costa Rica)

PART 2 *Using Transitions in the Conclusion*

Often a writer will use a word or phrase that signals to readers that they are moving from one thought to another, or from one section of a paper to another. These words are called transitions, and they are used to link ideas together. Some common transitions used to signal conclusions are listed below. The examples show how to use these transitions and how to punctuate them correctly.

Transitions:	In short,	Thus,	In conclusion,
	In summary,	Therefore,	To conclude,
	To summarize,		

Examples:

To introduce a quick summary of the main points:

> (In short, In summary, To summarize,) there are three main ways that people should prepare themselves for employment: Study the job market . . .

Often used in the last sentence of a conclusion:

> (Thus, Therefore,) one must have the proper training and necessary skills in order to find good employment.

May be used in both of the above ways:

> To conclude, In conclusion,

PRACTICE 2

Comparing Introductions and Conclusions

As you practice writing conclusions, use conclusion transitions. See if you can identify the similarities of form in the introductions and conclusions of these student papers. Then complete the outlines.
Follow the directions.

▼ Underline the thesis statement in the introduction and the ideas of the thesis statement in the conclusion.

▼ Star (*) the beginning of the hook and the tie.

▼ Circle the general comments in the introduction and any opinions, evaluations, or feelings in the conclusion.

▼ Draw a box around any transitions.

▼ Use the thesis statement to help you complete the missing parts of the planning outline.

Paper I: The Car—Good Fortune and Misfortune

Introduction

In 1885, Karl Benz, a forty-one-year-old German engineer, made the first car in the world. From that, humanity has entered the car stage. Roads the world over are crowded with cars. Cars take a person from place to place quickly. With cars, it is possible for people to work in the city and live in the countryside. Although cars are very useful, they cause noise, pollution, and serious accidents.

Conclusion

In conclusion, cars bring pleasure to millions of people, but also loud noise, pollution, and death. Since the making of the first car, cars have revolutionized our lives. Cars changed where people worked and lived. Cars changed what people did in their spare time. Cars became an important part of life, but their problems cannot be ignored. People are finding ways to deal with these problems. Someday other kinds of power will take the place of gasoline, and stricter laws will reduce the bad effects. Thus, because cars will always be with us, future cars must be noiseless and safer.

(Chening Zhang—People's Republic of China)

I. Introduction

II. _____

III. _____

IV. _____

V. _____

VI. Conclusion

Circle the type of comments in the conclusion: summary, evaluation, opinion.

Paper 2: Vulnerable Children

Introduction

Getting divorced nowadays has become as common as getting married. It is like buying wedding rings and then throwing them away. Still, for parents, it seems not to be a big problem. But for children it's more than a simple pair of rings. Children are devastated when they think they are at fault and often feel anger, loneliness, and depression, and have low self-esteem.

Conclusion

In short, children are still the most vulnerable part of the family and the effects of divorce on them are devastating. Children think they are at fault. They feel great anger, loneliness, depression, and low self-esteem. Considering what parents mean to their children and how much children need their parents, it is sad to see how divorce continues. It seems that many couples have forgotten that children are not just pretty rings.

(Rodolfo Peña—Mexico)

I. Introduction

II. _____

III. _____

IV. _____

V. _____

VI. Conclusion

Circle the type of comments in the conclusion: summary, evaluation, opinion.

Paper 3: People Should Not Smoke

Introduction

"Would you mind if I smoke?" I wanted to say, "Yes, I do mind," yet I said, "No, go ahead." Although I really hate the smell of smoke, and even seeing someone smoking, if the person politely asks my permission, I cannot say, "Do not smoke." In the past few years the bad effects of smoking have been scientifically proven. Still, there are a number of people who keep smoking. There are several good health reasons why people must not smoke.

Conclusion

People must not smoke for several reasons. Smoking causes many diseases that are serious and make people's lives shorter. For women, smoking influences the woman's child and her body. Also, the smoke from cigarettes gives even nonsmokers bad effects. Therefore, smokers should realize these awful facts and must quit smoking before they come down with a bad disease and die.

(Takako Kodani—Japan)

I. Introduction

II. _____

III. _____

IV. _____

V. Conclusion

Circle the type of comments in the conclusion: summary, evaluation, opinion.

Read the following essay about homeless people.

Follow the directions and write your own conclusion on a piece of paper.

PRACTICE 3

Writing a Conclusion

▼ Underline the thesis statement in the introduction.

▼ Underline the topic sentences in the second and third paragraphs.

▼ Write a conclusion. Remember to:

1. Restate the ideas in the thesis statement.

2. Use transitions.

3. Add comments using summary, evaluation, and/or opinion.

4. End with a final statement.

Street Beggars Are Not Always Homeless

Tom is a man who stands on a street corner with a ragged cardboard sign. "Homeless and Hungry—Please Help" is scrawled across the dirty cardboard in black Magic Marker. Tom said he is grateful for the people who give him money. "I don't force people to give me money," Tom said. "I just stand here and accept it. It's my way of making a living—this is America, the land of opportunity," he said. What drives people to stand on a street corner and beg? Some people like to beg, and others need to beg.

Some people pretend to be homeless when they really aren't. One example is Tom. He eventually admitted he has a house, but insisted he would lose his house if he did not panhandle for a living. "I need it to scrape by," Tom said. But scraping by for Tom means making $250 on really good days, and from $50 to $100 a day usually, he said. Another example is Frank, who also has a house. He is out asking people for money because he likes the freedom of his own hours and moving around whenever he wants to. Frank said he averages about $75 a day.

However, some people feel forced to beg. Ed is homeless, but he doesn't beg for money very often—only when he can't find an odd job to do. Willy lost his job in Oregon 20 years ago and has been on the road ever since. He doesn't have a job, car, or house. Brent Crane, the executive director of the Utah Valley Food and Shelter Coalition, said almost all of the needy are too proud to ask for handouts, but they will come to the shelter when they want help.

(Courtesy of The Daily Universe. *Adapted with permission.)*

_____

_____

_____

_____

_____

_____

_____

**Now you are ready to write a conclusion
to your cause-and-effect research paper for this unit.**

CHAPTER 11

Writing with Transitions

INTRODUCTION

Transitions are special words and phrases used in English, especially in formal writing. They show the logical relationship between sentences and ideas. Also, a transition sentence frequently is used to link one paragraph to the next paragraph.

Because academic papers use more formal language than other kinds of writing, you can expect to see more transitions in academic writing. Formal paragraphs often have as many as three transition words or phrases and sometimes more in long paragraphs.

In Chapter 10, you practiced using transitions in your conclusion. The conclusion transition signaled the reader that you were about to finish your essay. In this chapter you will study transitions that signal other meanings.

PART 1 *Frequently Used Transition Words and Phrases*

Here are groups of frequently used transition words with punctuation and example sentences of how they can be used. How many transition words in this list do you know how to use correctly?

For Additional Information:
and, also, too, another, furthermore, moreover, in addition

Sample Sentences

1. The country was in confusion, **and** the President couldn't do anything about it. The President decided to call a special session of Congress. He **also** wanted to call together some important political leaders.
2. He called the governors of the states, **too.**
3. **Another** group he called was the Cabinet.
4. The President decided to call a special session of Congress. **Furthermore, (Moreover, In addition,)** he was considering bringing the governors together.

For Clarification: in fact, as a matter of fact, that is, in other words

Sample Sentences:

1. There are some people who like Gloria Estefan. **In fact,** they adore her.
2. **As a matter of fact,** there are people who worship the ground she walks on.
3. **That is, (In other words,)** they follow after her, watch or keep track of her every move, buy every recording she makes, and organize Gloria Estefan fan clubs.

For Examples: for example, for instance, to illustrate, such as

Sample Sentences:

1. Firefighters must receive training to be effective. **For example, (For instance,)** they must learn how to protect themselves from various kinds of fires and how to rescue people from all sizes of buildings.
2. **To illustrate** their ability, the firefighters demonstrated rescuing people from high-rise buildings on the corner of Main and Center Streets yesterday at noon.
3. They did activities **such as** climbing tall ladders to open windows on the seventh floor, carrying stuffed figures down the ladders over their shoulders, and dropping the figures into safety nets.

For Contrast: in contrast, on the other hand, however, but

Sample Sentences:

1. A Porsche is an expensive car. **In contrast,** a Nissan is quite inexpensive.
2. A Mercedes is more comfortable than a Dodge. **On the other hand,** a Dodge is more economical.
3. A Ford is less expensive than a Mercedes; **however, (but)** it is not as comfortable.

For Cause: because . . . , since . . . , for this reason

Sample Sentences:

1. **Because (Since)** he got to class late, he started the final exam 30 minutes after the rest of the students.
2. He started the final exam 30 minutes after the rest of the students **because (since)** he got to class late.
3. He got to class late. **For this reason,** he started the final exam 30 minutes after the rest of the students.

For Effect: Consequently, As a consequence, As a result, ; therefore,

Sample Sentences:

1. **Consequently, (As a consequence, As a result,)** his grade was lower than he hoped.
2. He started the final exam late; **therefore,** his grade was lower than he hoped.

For Meaningful order:

First	Second	After	Last
First of all	Now	After that	Finally,
Before	Next	Later	Most important
One way	More important	Another way	

Sample Sentences:

1. Scientists try to explain why dinosaurs became extinct. **First, (First of all,)** they think the world became colder. **Second, (Next,)** they think the colder temperature destroyed many plants that dinosaurs ate. **Finally, (Last,)** they think dinosaurs didn't adapt to these new conditions.
2. **Before** scientists realized the big bones of dinosaurs were from an extinct group of animals, they thought they were mammoth bones. **After** they collected all the bones they could find, they put them together.
3. **Now** when scientists find dinosaur bones, they put them in plaster. **Later** they carefully take off the plaster and reconstruct the skeletons.
4. **One way** to take off the plaster is with small chisels. **Another way** is with soft brushes.
5. It is important to study fossil bones where they are found. **More important** is to study the position they are in and the surroundings of the site. **Most important** is to carefully preserve the bones for posterity.

See the Appendix (pp. 00-00) for a more complete list of transitions.

PRACTICE 1

Comparing Paragraphs with and without Transitions

▼ Read and compare paragraphs 1A with 1B and 2A with 2B.

▼ Circle the transitions.

▼ Write the meaning of each transition in the margin.

▼ Describe the differences you see between A and B. Which paragraph is easier to understand?

Paragraph 1

Apples

A. An economic reason for keeping apples in cold storage is the constant demand for them in the grocery store. Parents are still sending apples in school lunches in April and during the peak apple harvest season of September and October. Products made with fresh apples are in constant demand. If apples are too costly, the demand goes down. The cost of storing apples is spread over the total price charged year-round.

B. An economic reason for keeping apples in cold storage is the constant demand for them in the grocery store. For instance, parents are still sending apples in school lunches in April as often as during the peak apple harvest season of September and October. Furthermore, products made with fresh apples, such as apple pie and cakes, are in constant demand. However, if apples are too costly, the demand goes down. Consequently, the cost of storing apples is spread over the total price charged year-round.

Paragraph 2

Flu and Colds

A. When the cold and flu season hits, parents and children need all the help they can get. Children get colds about six times a year or more and get the flu at least once a year. Colds develop slowly with sneezing, stuffiness, runny nose, thick coughing, and a raspy sore throat. Sometimes children have a mild fever. Flu comes on very fast with sudden chills and fever, an upset stomach, and a headache. These seasonal illnesses are no fun for the parents. They are no fun for the children.

B. When the cold and flu season hits, parents and children need all the help they can get. As a matter of fact, children get colds about six times a year or more, and, similarly, get the flu at least once a year. Colds develop slowly with sneezing, stuffiness, runny nose, thick coughing, and a raspy sore throat. Furthermore, sometimes children have a mild fever. Flu, on the other hand, comes on very fast with sudden chills and fever, an upset stomach, and a headache. These seasonal illnesses are no fun for either the parents or the children.

PRACTICE 2

Adding Transitions

▼ Read the paragraphs that follow.

▼ Rewrite each paragraph on a piece of paper and add transitions.

▼ Be sure to keep the writer's meaning.

▼ Use correct punctuation.

Paragraph 1

Vaccines

Parents usually try to keep their children safe from different dangers common in our day. Violence, drugs, immorality, delinquency, and other bad habits are some factors. There is a danger, an invisible but real danger, called *viruses*, that can attack without any notice. Specific vaccines can be used in order to avoid diseases caused by viruses. These vaccines can start in childhood as early as the second month of life and can be given through adulthood. Immunization is the only way to protect against this invisible but real danger.

Paragraph 2

A Blind Date

A *blind date* is a date with a person you haven't met. Some people are too shy to meet a boyfriend or girlfriend. They need help. A friend calls a shy friend and says, "I know a wonderful person, and I think you two would get along. Would you let me make a date for you to go together to the next baseball game?" These two strangers go on a date together. It can be terrible. It can be a waste of time. It can be fun. It can be the first step to meeting your marriage partner. You will never know unless you decide to try it.

Now you are ready to add transitions to your cause-and-effect research paper. Use the list of frequently used transitions to help you.

Preparing the Final Paper

In Chapters 9 through 11 you worked on writing your cause-and-effect research paper. You should have a good introduction and conclusion prepared with meaningful transitions. After you revise and rewrite, and edit and rewrite to your satisfaction, you are ready to combine the parts of the paper. These parts are:

- the title page
- the final outline
- the research paper
- the reference list

All of the parts of your final paper should be put in a folder in this order.

PART 1 *The Title Page*

The first page of your paper is the title page. For this assignment you will use the traditional title page. Look back at page 18 to see how to type a traditional title page. Remember to use capital letters for the first letter of all important words in the title. Do not use all capital letters.

> **Now you can type the title page for your research paper.**

P A R T 2 *From Planning Outline to Final Outline*

1. A **planning outline** is the plan that the writer makes to organize all the information *before* beginning to write. It can be as simple as putting numbers next to the information on a sheet of paper to show the order in which the information will be used.

2. A **final outline** helps the reader understand how you organized the material in the paper. This final outline is prepared *after* the paper is written and revised for the last time.

Examine the form for the final outline of a research paper. Notice that it has the title *Outline* at the top. Also notice that the outline is single-spaced.

Outline

I. Introduction
    A. (Hook—To catch the attention of your reader)
    B. (General comments on the topic)
    C. (Thesis statement—Gives the topic and parts of the topic)

II. (First major division)
    A.
        1.
        2.
    B.
        1.
            a.
            b.
        2.

III. (Second major division)
    A.
    B.
        1.
        2.

IV. (Third major division)
    A.
        1.
        2.
    B.

V. Conclusion
    A. (Restatement of the ideas in the thesis statement)
    B. (Summary, opinion, and/or evaluation of topic parts)
    C. (Final statement to close or *tie* the paper for the reader)

3. Compare the following examples of a planning outline and a final outline. Which parts are the same in both outlines? Which parts are left out of the final outline? Which parts are more complete in the final outline? Where are there complete sentences in the final outline?

PLANNING OUTLINE

I. Introduction
    War—mass rape
    Who makes the decisions?
        government
        religion
        individuals
II. Legal points of view
    Ireland
    United States
III. Religious points of view
    Muslim
    Catholic
    Protestant
    Mormon
    Jewish
    Buddhist
IV. Conclusion
    Rape is horrible
    Should be a crime

FINAL OUTLINE

I. Introduction
    A. Pregnancy that is a result
       of rape is a dilemma
       in most countries.

    B. WW II
       1. Mass rape
       2. Political/Religious motives

    C. Opinions about pregnancy
       due to rape vary with
       governments and religions.

II. Governments' views
    A. Hungary—allows abortion
    B. Poland—limited abortion
    C. Ireland—no legal abortion
    D. USA
       1. States vary
       2. California law compared to
          Utah law
III. Religious views
    A. Muslim—no abortion
    B. Catholic—no abortion
    C. Protestant—varies
    D. Mormon—limited abortion
    E. Jewish—varies
    F. Buddhist—varies
IV. Conclusion
    A. Governments and religions
       affect opinions about rape
    B. Summary of government and
       religious views
    C. Rape is wrong in any society

P A R T 3 *Typing the Research Paper*

1. **Typing the paper.** Type on one side of 8 1/2 x 11 inch white paper.

2. **Margins.** Leave a one-inch margin on all four sides of your paper. If you use a typewriter, you will need to set the margins on the left- and right-hand sides to leave one inch and begin typing one inch from the top on each paper. You should also leave one inch at the bottom of each page.

If you use a computer, the word-processing program is probably already set for a one-inch margin. This means that your work will automatically be printed on the paper with one-inch margins.

3. **Font.** Use a traditional font for typing your paper. Do not use all italics, bold, or capitals. Make sure the words are big enough to read easily (12 point).

4. **Spacing.** Double-space the entire paper. Don't add extra line spaces between paragraphs. Indent five spaces at the beginning of each paragraph. You can use a tab if it is set for five spaces. If you are using a word processor, add a space between sentences and after a comma, a colon, or a semicolon. If you are using a regular typewriter, add two spaces between sentences, and one space after a comma, a colon, or a semicolon.

5. **Title of paper.** The title is typed on the first page of the paper. It is centered between the left and right margins. Double-space and begin typing your introduction.

6. **Short Title.** APA style requires that the first two or three words of your title be put in the upper right-hand corner of each page. This is called the short title. Do not type the complete title unless it is short.

7. **Page Numbers.** The page number in APA style is in the upper right-hand corner, double-spaced under the short title. Double-space after the page number to continue typing your paper.

Example:

Effects of Television Violence

3

The Effects of Television Violence on Children

"Television is not reflecting the world, but the world is reflecting television" (Brady, 1992, p. 50). Television is the most widespread media that brings violence to our youngsters,

---

Effects of Television Violence

4

hurt people, you get what you want" is the message TV shows may project.

As well as teaching violence as power, TV also presents violence as the only way to solve problems. Children see on TV how, time after time, violence brings solutions to problems. "If they see characters they enjoy watching using violence

PART 4 *Typing the Reference List*

The reference list includes the sources of the information in your paper. The sources are in alphabetical order according to the first word of each reference. The first line of each source is at the left margin of the page, and all other lines are indented.

Each entry must follow exactly the APA style for the kind of article it represents. See the Appendix (pg. 235) for a more complete list of reference forms.

References in APA Style

1. Encyclopedia article

(Note: Encyclopedias are seldom used as references in college research papers.)

Form: Author's last name, initials. (year). Title of article. In name of first editor et al. (Eds.), <u>Name of Encyclopedia</u> (Vol. #, page number/s). Place published: Name of publisher.

Example: Pixton, E. A. (1980). Cotton production. In J. Smith et al. (Eds.), <u>Encyclopedia of Economy</u> (Vol. 3, pp. 952–953). London: Blackwell & Sons, Ltd.

2. Encyclopedia article, no author

Form: Title of article. (year). In name of first editor et al. (Eds.), <u>Name of Encyclopedia</u> (Vol. #, page number/s). Place published: Name of publisher.

Example: Cotton. (1985). In N. Yeld et al. (Eds.), <u>William's Encyclopedia</u> (Vol. 4, p. 850). New York: Littleton Press.

3. Professional journal article

Form: Author's last name, initials. (year). Title of article. <u>Name of Journal</u>, Vol. #, page numbers.

Example: Paivio, A. (1975). Perceptual comparisons through the mind's eye. <u>Memory & Cognition</u>, 3, 635–647.

4. Magazine article

Form: Author's last name, initial/s. (year, month day). Title of article. <u>Name of Magazine</u>, page numbers.

Example: Johnson, J. (1991, June 13). Is America becoming dishonest? <u>Men and Women Today</u>, pp. 70–76.

5. Newspaper article

Form: Author's last name, initials. (year, month day). Title of article. <u>Name of Newspaper</u>, page number.

Example: O'Leary, K. (1992, February 14). Ethical decisions a part of everyday existence, speaker tells students. <u>The Daily Universe</u>, p. 4.

6. Newspaper article, no author

Form: Title of article. (year, month day). <u>Name of Newspaper</u>, page number.

Example: Bush outlines aid to former republics. (1992, April 2). <u>Langley Gazette</u>, p. B1.

Sample reference list

These examples are the same references as those given on pages 102 and 103. Now they are written in alphabetical order. How is a source listed when there is no author?

Perceptual Comparisons

12

References

Bush outlines aid to former republics. (1992, April 2). <u>Langley Gazette</u>, p. B1.

Cotton. (1985). In N. Yeld et al. (Eds.), <u>William's Encyclopedia</u> (Vol. 4, p. 850). New York: Littleton Press.

Johnson, J. (1991, June). Is America becoming dishonest? <u>Men and Women Today</u>, pp. 70–76.

O'Leary, K. (1992, February 14). Ethical decisions a part of everyday existence, speaker tells students. <u>The Daily Universe</u>, p. 4.

Now you are ready to type your reference list. Place your notes, photocopied articles, and the first draft of your title page, outline, paper, and reference list in a folder to be evaluated by a classmate and then by the teacher.

Peer Evaluation of Cause-and-Effect Research Paper

▼ Put an *S* (Satisfactory) or a *U* (Unsatisfactory) on the blank in front of each item.

▼ Write the total number of *S*'s and *U*'s.

▼ Write any suggestions below. Use polite expressions.

Name of writer _____   Total S's _____

Name of evaluator_____   Total U's_____

Date_____

Title Page

_____ 1. Title page is in the correct form.

Outline

_____ 2. Has the title *Outline*.

_____ 3. Uses the correct numbers and letters.

_____ 4. Has logical categories.

_____ 5. Is in the student's own words.

Paper

_____ 6. The introduction has a hook.

_____ 7. The background information defines, explains, or gives facts that stay with the topic.

_____ 8. There is a clear thesis statement. (Underline the thesis statement.)

_____ 9. The paper is at least four handwritten pages or three typed pages.

_____ 10. The paper has margins on all four sides of the pages.

_____ 11. The paper is written on only one side of each page.

_____ 12. The paper is double-spaced (every other line).

_____ 13. New paragraphs are indented.

_____ 14. Each paragraph in the paper has a topic sentence.

_____ 15. The order of the paper matches the order of the outline.

_____ 16. Each page has a short title and a page number.

_____ 17. The conclusion restates the thesis statement.

_____ 18. The conclusion summarizes the body of the paper.

_____ 19. The conclusion has a good final sentence.

_____ 20. The paper was interesting to read.

Reference list

_____ 21. The bibliography has the title *References*.

_____ 22. The reference list has at least two sources, listed in alphabetical order.

_____ 23. The sources are in correct APA style.

Optional for first draft

_____ 24. The report is in a three-hole folder with student's name on the cover.

_____ 25. The report is in the correct order: title page, outline, paper, reference list.

_____ 26. The note cards and photocopies are in the pocket of the folder.

Tell the writer what you liked about this paper. Give some suggestions that might improve the paper.

Expanding Research Skills

In this unit, you will work on your research skills as you learn to write a comparison-and-contrast research paper. For this, you will need to learn to expand the sources you are using for research and then learn how to organize the information you have gathered in ways that will allow you to answer the questions "How are these things the same or similar?" and "How are these things different from one another?" You will also learn about the principles of academic honesty. It is very important in academic writing that you learn to give credit to the sources from which you take information. It is also extremely important that you learn how to avoid plagiarism—taking someone else's ideas or words and making your reader believe that they are your own.

In this unit you will:

▼ Learn how to write a comparison-and-contrast research paper

▼ Learn models for comparing and contrasting information

▼ Learn how to find other sources for research

▼ Learn how to make formal note cards while you do research

▼ Learn how to use information from other authors

You will also learn:

▼ How to use Venn diagrams and idea maps

▼ The principles of academic honesty

▼ What plagiarism means and how to avoid it by using citations

Other skills you will practice are:

▼ Paraphrasing, summarizing, and quoting

▼ Writing citations

▼ Creating a thesis statement from a research question

Preparing for Comparison-and-Contrast Research

INTRODUCTION

What is the meaning of comparison and contrast? To compare means to see what certain things have in common. We ask: "How are these items the same or similar?" To contrast means to look at several things to see how they are not the same. We ask: "How are these things different from each other?" We make comparisons between all sorts of things in our daily lives.

To compare and contrast accurately, you must look at details very carefully. Then you must decide which details are the same and which details are different.

PART 1 *Comparing and Contrasting Using a Venn Diagram*

One way of seeing comparisons and contrasts is to create a Venn diagram. A Venn diagram helps to show the similarities and differences between items. It looks like this:

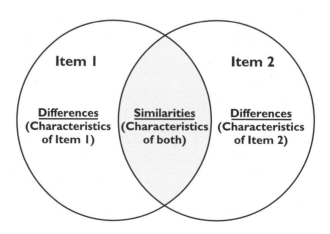

1. As a class, use a Venn diagram on the board to identify the similarities and the differences between these two garden photos.

2. Look at these two photos of a woman at a piano. Use the Venn diagram on the next page to list the similarities and differences.

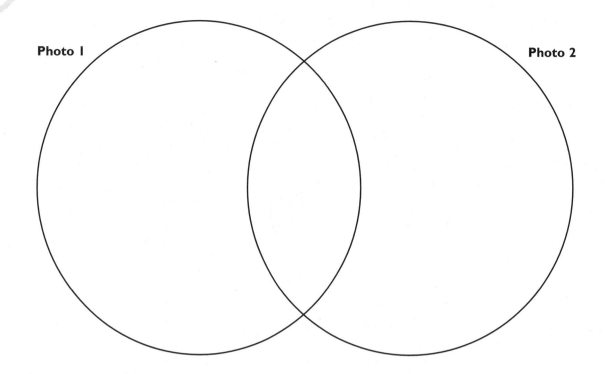

Photo 1   **Photo 2**

3. Look carefully at the shoes you are now wearing. What do they look like? Look at the picture below and compare the shoes you are wearing now to the shoe in this drawing. Look at the names of the parts of the shoe. Decide which parts of your shoes are the same and which parts are different from the shoe in the picture.

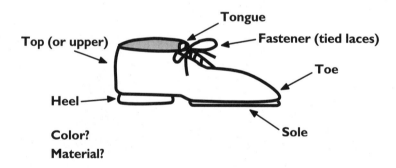

Color?
Material?

4. Compare your shoes to a classmate's shoes. Look carefully at the details. Here are some details to consider.

Content vocabulary

Top or upper	Heel	Sole	Tongue	Toe
Low cut	Low	Thin	Narrow	Pointed
Medium cut	Medium	Thick	Medium	Rounded
High cut	High	Wide	Wide	Wide
	Narrow	Hard	Padded	Flat
	Wide	Soft	Lined	High
	Stacked	Treaded		Open
	Spiked	Spikes		Closed

Decoration	*Color*	*Fastener*	*Material*	*Use*
Cut out	Black	Laces	Leather	Sports
Perforated	Brown	Buckle	Plastic	Dress
Trim stitching	White	Snap	Cloth	Casual
Glued parts	Maroon	Velcro	Vinyl	
Brand name	Tan	Zipper		
Overlay parts	Gray	Elastic		
Logo	Navy			

5. Write the similarities and differences between your shoes and a class-mate's in the Venn diagram below.

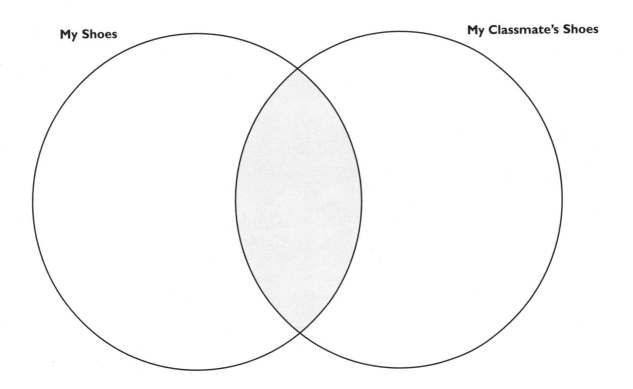

My Shoes

My Classmate's Shoes

PART 2 *Comparison-and-Contrast Model 1*

Here is a basic model of a comparison-and-contrast essay.

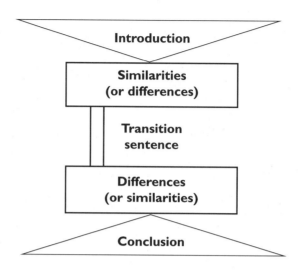

In the example below, notice the <u>underlined</u> words and phrases and the transitional sentence in **bold** type that show comparison-and-contrast relationships.

> The sun and the moon are similar <u>because</u> they are <u>both</u> round, above the earth, and they both show light. They are easy to see if the sky is clear, <u>and so</u> all people on the earth know the sun and the moon exist.

> **Even though the sun and the moon are similar in some ways, they are also very different.** The sun produces light by many explosions of gases. <u>However</u>, the moon only reflects light. The sun is <u>farther</u> away from the earth <u>than</u> the moon. <u>Also</u>, the sun gives light and heat for daytime. <u>In contrast</u>, the moon shines at night, <u>but</u> gives no heat.

PART 3 *Comparison-and-Contrast Transitions*

1. Comparison words and phrases:

Between sentences or paragraphs

Similarly,   Likewise,   Also,

Sample Sentences:

> 1. Both of the men are tall, dark, and handsome. **Similarly, (Likewise, Also,)** both of their wives are tall, dark, and beautiful.

Between words and phrases within the paragraph

(just) like	both . . . and	alike	similar (to)
the same (as)	not only . . . but also	compared to	so . . . that

Sample Sentences:

1. The men looked **just like** brothers. They **both** had blond, wavy hair **and** piercing blue eyes. They looked **so** much alike **that** from a distance we could not tell them apart. Actually they were more **similar** than some twins I once knew. They even acted **similar** to each other. **Not only** did they act and look **alike, but** they **also** had same-sounding voices. It was very confusing!

2. Contrast words and phrases:

Between sentences or paragraphs

On the other hand,   In contrast,   However,

Sample Sentences:

1. **On the other hand,** these two men are different in some aspects. John has a quiet nature and is sensitive. **In contrast,** Sam is loud and is concerned mostly about himself.

Between words and phrases within the paragraph

although	while	but	differ from
though	whereas	more than	different from
even though	yet	-er (than)	unlike

Sample Sentences:

1. Some of their differences are not very obvious. **Although** they both have blue eyes, Sam's eyes are dark blue and John's are powder blue. **Even though** they are both tall, John is slimm**er than** Sam, who has a rounder waist. Also, John's nose is **different from** Sam's because Sam's nose is long**er** and wid**er**. **Yet,** the biggest differences are in their personalities. John's nature is most **unlike** Sam's because he is soft-spoken and gentle, **whereas** Sam is loud and sure of himself. Also, the way John handles problems **differs from** Sam's. John is methodical and careful, **while** Sam is impulsive in all his decisions.

PRACTICE 1

Finding Transitions

▼ Read the following essay comparing three types of tuna.

▼ Circle the words and phrases that show comparison and contrast.

▼ Complete the outline at the end of the essay.

Tuna Anyone?

Tuna is one of the most common fish that people eat, and just like most foods, there are different types of tuna. There is white tuna, light tuna, and also a diet tuna. These types of tuna have only one similarity and four differences.

The only thing two of them have in common is the number of calories they have. Water-packed tuna, both light and diet, has about 100 calories per serving. However, oil-packed tuna (when the oil is drained off) has about 145 calories.

These fish differ in the species of tuna used, the flavor, the color, and the style of packing. White tuna must be made from albacore, which tastes like chicken and is very light, almost white, in color. Light tuna, however, is a mixture of yellowfin, skipjack, bigeye, and bluefin, which are darker in color and have a definite fish taste. Diet tuna, on the other hand, can be made with either white or light tuna and is tasteless and dry. Furthermore, white tuna is usually solid-packed in cans, light tuna is packed in chunks, and diet tuna is packed in small pieces.

At the store, the type of tuna that is chosen depends mostly on the customers' tastes. If they prefer the mild taste, they might pick the white tuna. If they prefer a fishy flavor, maybe the light will be for them. But if they are more concerned about calories, they would pick water-packed or diet tuna. In this world of choices, it is good that customers can pick from these three types of tuna.

Outline

I. Introduction

II. _____

III. _____

IV. Conclusion

PRACTICE 2

Using Comparison-and-Contrast Transitions

▼ Look at the Venn diagram you made on p. 109 when you compared two different types of shoes.

▼ Write one paragraph about the similarities and one about differences.

▼ Include a transition sentence and other comparison-and-contrast words from the chart.

P A R T 4 *More Comparison-and-Contrast Models*

For Model 1, you read comparisons of the sun and the moon and of three types of tuna. You also practiced comparing two types of shoes. You discussed the similarities in one paragraph and the differences in another.

There are two other models that are common in comparison-and-contrast essays. They are used for more complex topics that require a longer paper. Look carefully at these models.

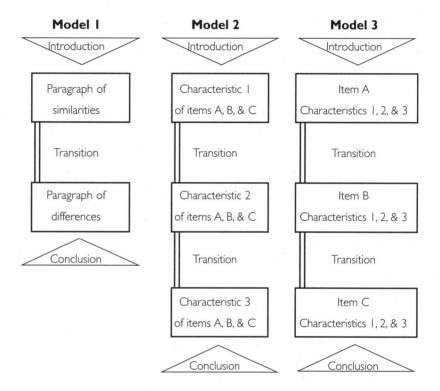

Sample paper using Model 2

As you read this paper, write the main idea of each paragraph in the margin. Circle all the transitions and transition sentences.

Haydn, Mozart, and Beethoven

Haydn, Mozart, and Beethoven were the greatest composers of the 18th century. They knew each other. In fact, Haydn influenced Mozart's music, and he was one of Beethoven's teachers. Even though they associated with each other, they had their own lives. Mozart died earlier than the other two, and Beethoven was deaf. Therefore, it is interesting to compare their musical educations, working styles, and achievements.

These three composers had some differences in their musical education. Haydn was born in an ordinary farmhouse (Elson, 1972), liked to sing songs with his parents, and mimic playing the violin. His father wanted him to be a musician, so he entered music school at age six (Prarry, 1972). Like Haydn, Mozart's family was also musical. His father was a good violinist (Elson, 1972). At an early age Mozart could remember tunes and recognize easy chords on the harpsichord (Parry, 1972). But unlike Haydn, who went to school at an early age, Mozart started composing at age five (Elson, 1972) and performing at age six (Parry, 1972). Although Beethoven was also born into a musical family, his music education began later in his childhood. A chapel organist taught him to play the organ and he became a cymbalist in a theater orchestra at age twelve.

Their working styles were more different than their education. Haydn liked a calm, quiet place to work, and he always wore neat, clean clothes while he was composing (Parry, 1972). In contrast, Mozart didn't care where he composed. According to Konard (1992), "He was able to jot down whatever works he liked, whenever he liked, wherever he happened to be" (p. 121). He even composed while he was playing billiards (Elson, 1972). Beethoven's style was not like Haydn's or Mozart's. Beethoven was only able to compose when he felt strong emotions (Parry, 1972). Sometimes these moments happened even when he was taking a walk (Elson, 1972).

The achievements of these three composers were also different. Although they all composed instrumental music, Haydn tried to use different instruments together to make rich sounds. He was also the founder of secular music, because he was interested in different people's songs and dances (Elson, 1972). Mozart's musical emphasis was different from Haydn's. He wrote music for symphonies, concertos, and string quartets. He also developed sacred music (Ardoin, 1989). Beethoven, however, worked to join the intellectual part of music with the emotions (Elson, 1972). To do this, he changed the traditional use of the instruments and enlarged their scale (Parry, 1972).

In conclusion, Haydn, Mozart, and Beethoven had different musical educations, working styles, and achievements. Their lives, their compositions, and their greatness came out of all these features, and they used their talents faithfully. Even though there are many other composers in the world, these three will remain the greatest of the 18th century.

(Jihee Kim—Korea)

Sample paper using Model 3

Here is the same information about Haydn, Mozart, and Beethoven, written to follow Model 3. Write the main idea of each paragraph in the left margin. What are some other differences or similarities between the two papers?

Haydn, Mozart, and Beethoven

Haydn, Mozart, and Beethoven were the greatest composers of the eighteenth century. They knew each other. In fact, Haydn influenced Mozart's music, and he was one of Beethoven's teachers. Even though they associated with each other, they had their own lives. Mozart died earlier than the other two, and Beethoven was deaf. Therefore, it is interesting to compare their musical educations, working styles, and achievements.

Haydn was born in an ordinary farmhouse (Elson, 1972), liked to sing songs with his parents, and mimic playing the violin. His father wanted him to be a musician, so he entered music school at age six. Haydn liked a calm, quiet place to work, and he always wore neat, clean clothes while he was composing (Parry, 1972). Haydn tried to use different instruments together to make rich sounds. He was also the founder of secular music, because he was interested in different people's songs and dances (Elson, 1972).

Like Haydn, Mozart's family was also musical. His father was a good violinist (Elson, 1972). At an early age Mozart could remember tunes and recognize easy chords on the harpsichord (Parry, 1972). But unlike Haydn, who went to school at an early age, Mozart started composing at age five (Elson, 1972) and performing at age six (Parry, 1972). Also, Mozart didn't care where he composed. According to Konard (1992), "He was able to jot down whatever works he liked, whenever he liked, wherever he happened to be" (p. 121). He even composed while he was playing billiards (Elson, 1972). Furthermore, Mozart's musical emphasis was different from Haydn's. He wrote music for symphonies, concertos, and string quartets. He also developed sacred music (Ardoin, 1989).

Similarly, Beethoven was also born into a musical family, but his formal education in music began later in his childhood. A chapel organist taught him to play the organ and he became a cymbalist in a theater orchestra at age twelve. Beethoven's style was not like Haydn's or Mozart's. Beethoven was only able to compose when he felt strong emotions (Parry, 1972). Sometimes these moments happened even when he was taking a walk (Elson, 1972). Beethoven's achievements were also a little different from those of the other two composers. He worked to join the intellectual part of music with the emotions (Elson, 1972). To do this, he changed the traditional use of the instruments and enlarged their scale (Parry, 1972).

In conclusion, Haydn, Mozart, and Beethoven had different musical educations, working styles, and achievements. Their lives, their compositions, and their greatness came out of all these features, and they used their talents faithfully. Even though there are many other composers in the world, these three will remain the greatest of the 18th century.

PRACTICE 3

Analyzing Comparison-and-Contrast Essays

Finding mistakes in the organization of an essay can help you learn how to write a better paper.

▼ Read each of the essays below. Look carefully at the thesis statement. Examine the rest of the essay.

▼ Write the parts that are missing or weak on the line below each essay. (Example: *"has weak thesis statement"* or *"is missing information about the cost of tuna"*)

▼ Explain which comparison-and-contrast model was used.

Essay 1

Tuna is probably the most common form of food from the ocean. In order to satisfy different tastes, it is canned in three different types. In comparing these types we must consider the number of calories, the taste, and the price of each.

Each type of tuna has different calories, depending on if it is packed in oil or water. White tuna has about 100 calories per serving if it is canned in water, and 145 calories if canned in oil. Light tuna, packed in oil, has a few more calories than white if packed in oil and eaten drained. Diet tuna is always packed in water, and the number of calories is similar to light tuna.

The three types of tuna have very different flavors. White tuna, which is mostly made of a mild-tasting albacore tuna, tastes like chicken. On the other hand, light tuna, a mixture of various tunas, has a stronger fish taste than albacore. Diet tuna is tasteless since there is no salt added. It is also dry.

The missing part/s:

_____

_____

The writer was following Model _____.

_____

Essay 2

What are white, light, and diet tunas? We use them every day without being aware of their similarities and differences. The only similarity is that they are made from fish.

As for differences, their flavors are different. The flavor of white tuna is chicken-like, light tuna has a stronger fish taste, and diet tuna is bland and dry and not too tasty. Also, they have different prices. White tuna costs $1.50 per can, light tuna is about $0.75 a can, and diet tuna is as expensive as white. They are also packed in different liquids. White and light are packed in oil or water, and diet is packed only in water.

Therefore, the three tunas have similarities and differences.

The weak parts:

_____

_____

The writer was following Model _____.

Writing a Comparison-and-Contrast Research Paper

INTRODUCTION

So far in this unit on comparison and contrast, you have learned:

▼ how to use a Venn diagram in preparation for the paper

▼ transition words and phrases that show comparison and contrast

▼ three models for a research paper

PART 1 *Unit Four Assignment: Comparison-and-Contrast Research Paper*

Now you are ready to begin a comparison-and-contrast research paper. The rest of this unit will teach you new skills as you work step by step through this assignment. While you work through the writing process of this paper, you will learn how to:

● narrow a comparison-and-contrast topic

● change a research question to a thesis statement

● choose information for a report

● paraphrase, summarize, and quote parts of the information

● make note cards

● write citations

The following assignment will act as a map to the final draft of your paper. By the time you complete this unit, you will be ready to hand in the final draft of your paper.

I. GETTING STARTED   Due: _____

    A. Choose your own topic with the teacher's approval or select one of these topics:

        Types of: homes, insects, flowers, birds, food, energy, holidays

        Different: actors, singers, authors, musical groups

        Example: Types of insects: Ants, Bees, and Wasps

        Actors: Charlie Chaplin, Whoopi Goldberg, and Bill Cosby

    B. Narrow your topic by using a Venn diagram or an idea map (see p. 000) to help you choose the areas to compare and contrast.

    C. Create a possible research question for your topic. Write it on the lines below.

My research question is:

_____

_____

II. PREWRITING

    A. Brainstorm about your narrowed topic.

    B. Revise your research question as necessary.

III. GATHERING INFORMATION (two sources)   Due: _____

    A. Find a magazine (periodical) article

        1. Use the computer catalog or *The Reader's Guide to Periodical Literature*.

        2. Copy the bibliographic information on a 3 × 5 card or print it out from the computer.

        3. Make a photocopy of the article.

    B. Find a book that will give you information.

        1. In the computer catalog, find the titles of a few books that might have some information.

        2. Quickly scan the table of contents, looking for a part that will answer the research question.

        3. Make a photocopy of the part you need.

        4. Write the bibliographic information for the book on a 3 × 5 card.

    C. Read, underline, and make marginal notes on the photocopies. Do not write in the library book.

    D. As you find information, you might have to change some of the points of your first research question.

IV. ORGANIZING YOUR INFORMATION   Due: _____

    A. Transfer marginal notes you want to use onto 3 × 5 cards.

        1. Write one marginal note per card.
        2. Follow the correct form for note cards.

    B. Organize the cards and write your planning outline.

    C. Change your thesis statement if necessary.

V. WRITING YOUR FIRST DRAFT   Due: _____

    A. Write the comparison-and-contrast paper from your outline.

        1. Create a citation for each paraphrase, summary, or quotation in your paper.
        2. Use transitions between groups of information.

    B. Write a title page and a reference list.

    C. Write your final outline.

VI. REVISING AND REWRITING (more drafts)   Due: _____

    A. Add details, examples, and explanations if necessary to make the meaning clear to the reader.

    B. Reorganize if necessary.

    C. Improve paragraphing and topic sentences if necessary.

VII. EDITING AND REWRITING (final draft)   Due: _____

    A. Read your paper aloud.

    B. Correct errors in grammar, spelling, and punctuation.

    C. Use the spell-check feature on your word processor.

Preparing the folder to turn in:

    A. Put your completed research paper in a three-hole pocket folder. Make sure that the pages are in this order.

        1. Title page
        2. Final outline
        3. Research paper
        4. Reference list

    B. Place these items in the pockets of the folder:

        1. Photocopies of articles
        2. Note cards with a rubber band around them
        3. First draft of the paper
        4. The other drafts of your paper

PART 2   *Narrowing Your Topic*

In the first step of writing a research paper, you must make sure that your topic is narrow enough to handle in a three-page paper and yet broad enough to be interesting. One mistake many students make is beginning a research paper with a topic that is too broad. This can cause confusion when they begin to do the research. Here are research questions that are too broad. Why are they too broad?

1. "What are the differences and similarities between methods of transportation?"

2. "What are the differences between American schools and Mexican schools?"

3. "What are the differences and similarities among communication systems?"

4. "How are France and Spain alike?"

5. "What are the differences between the European Common Market and the American free-market system?"

Narrowing a comparison-and-contrast topic and research question can be done in a Venn diagram or in an idea map.

1. Venn Diagram

You have learned that a Venn diagram can be used to illustrate similarities and differences between two specific things. This diagram can be used to narrow a comparison-and-contrast topic as well. For example, if your general topic is "flowers" and you are specifically interested in "roses" and "pansies," the Venn diagram and the final research question might look like this:

Topic: Flowers

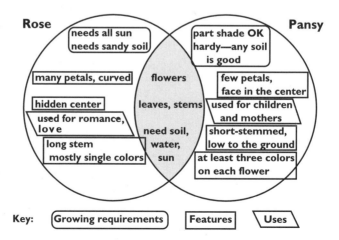

Rose

needs all sun
needs sandy soil

many petals, curved

hidden center

used for romance, love

long stem
mostly single colors

flowers
leaves, stems
need soil, water, sun

Pansy

part shade OK
hardy—any soil is good

few petals, face in the center

used for children and mothers

short-stemmed, low to the ground

at least three colors on each flower

Key: Growing requirements   Features   Uses

Narrowed research question:

How are the physical features, the growing requirements, and the uses of roses and pansies similar and different?

If you want to compare and contrast three items or people, you would use a Venn diagram with three overlapping circles.

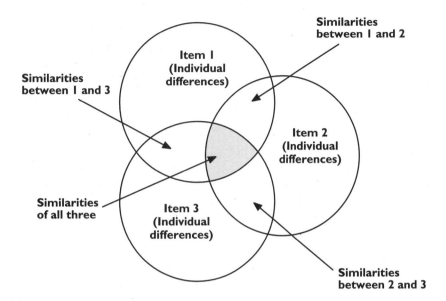

2. Idea Map

An idea map is a general topic centered on a paper with ideas or facts grouped around it. For example, if you chose "transportation" you might begin by narrowing it to "cars." To narrow your topic further, write the word "cars" in the middle of a piece of paper. Quickly list all the items related to cars. Try to group ideas or facts. When you cannot think of anything else to write down, look at the items and pick out a few that would be interesting to compare and contrast.

Look at the following example of an idea map to see how it helped a student decide on a narrowed research question.

Topic: transportation

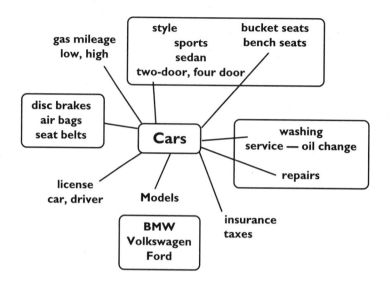

Narrowed research question:

**What are the differences and the similarities
between a Volkswagen, a Ford, and a BMW in their
body style, care, and safety?**

> **In your notebook, use a Venn diagram or an idea map to narrow the
> topic for your comparison-and-contrast research paper.
> Write a narrowed research question.**

PART 3   *From Final Research Question to a Thesis Statement*

Look at these two examples of comparison-and-contrast research questions
and thesis statements. Notice how each thesis statement restates the research
question. Which thesis statement is specific and which one is general?

1. **Research Question** What are the differences and similarities between
   a VW and a BMW in their body style, care, and
   safety?

   Thesis Statement The VW and BMW are vastly different cars with
   very little in common.

2. **Research Question** How are the physical features, propagation, and
   uses of roses and pansies similar and different?

   Thesis Statement Although the rose and the pansy are both flowers
   gardeners plant frequently, they are quite different
   in their physical features, growing requirements,
   and uses.

PRACTICE 1

Writing Thesis Statements
from Research Questions

▼ Read the following research questions.

▼ Write a thesis statement for each.

1. **Research Question:** Which colleges offer the best courses in engineering?

   Thesis Statement: _____, _____, and _____ are the best colleges for engineering majors.

2. **Research Question:** How do the styles, colors, and uses of traditional women's costumes of Korea, Japan, and Taiwan compare?

   Thesis Statement:

   _____

   _____

3. **Research Question:** What are the differences between modern jazz and new wave music in rhythm, melody, and instruments?

   Thesis Statement:

   _____

   _____

> **Now write the research question and thesis statement for your comparison-and-contrast research paper.**

Research Question:

_____

_____

Thesis Statement:

_____

_____

PART 4 *Guidelines for Choosing Information*

1. First go to the index books or a computer terminal and look up your topic. Topics are in alphabetical order.

   a. Look at the titles that you find.

   b. Read any abstracts or summary statements in brackets [ ] next to the title if there is no abstract.

c. Ask: "Which reading might answer my research question?"

2. Next, choose a number of readings (five to ten) that seem as if they may have the information you want.

   a. Write down the bibliographic information for each one. This will help you find the article or book and will help you when you write your reference list.

   b. Copy the book's call number. This number will help you find the location of the reading in your library.

   c. Look carefully to see if there is any other important information, such as additional key words that will direct you to other useful articles.

Note: Make sure you get all the reference information before you leave the library!

3. Next, look for the location of the readings in the library by using the call number. Follow the library maps or ask a librarian.

4. When you find the articles and books, scan them quickly.

   a. The purpose of scanning is to:

      • See if there is any part that seems to answer your research question. If not, find another source.

      • Look at the vocabulary. If it is so hard you can't understand the main ideas, find another source.

      • Judge how many answers to your research question you may find in that reading. If the article will help only a little, find other readings, too.

   b. To scan an article, quickly read the abstract and subtitles. If there are no abstracts or subtitles, look at the first and last paragraphs. Then look at the beginning sentences of several paragraphs.

   c. To scan a book, look through the table of contents and the index.

5. Select some readings to use for your report.

   a. Select only those readings, or parts of readings, that seem to answer your research question.

   b. Check out the book from the library or photocopy the part you will use for your notes.

PRACTICE 2

Choosing Information to Answer a Research Question

▼ For each topic below, read the two related articles.

▼ Underline only those parts that answer the research question.

▼ Make a marginal note that summarizes each underlined part.

▼ Be prepared to discuss why you chose those parts.

TOPIC 1: "What are the differences between modern alarms and traditional alarms?"

Useful Alarms

Consider the different types of alarms that are useful every day. There are silent alarms. For instance, on the seacoast a lighthouse uses a strong ray of light to warn boats about a dangerous place on the shore. In a bank, a silent alarm may be an electronic field. This field consists of beams of light that go across a room. If anything disturbs the beam, like a burglar at night or an unauthorized person approaching the safe, a signal goes off. At night this signal is often transferred to a nearby police station. Another silent alarm is smoke. Smoke can tell you where there is a fire. In the past, Native Americans used controlled smoke signals from the mountain tops to inform people of danger or important meetings. However, the most common type of alarm is a bell, either mechanical or electrical. Students soon learn that they are late if the school bell rings and they are not in class. In addition, bells tell us to get out of the way when a fire truck, ambulance, or police car is passing swiftly by. Also, the ringing of a telephone sends us quickly to the phone to find out who is calling. Probably the most distasteful alarm is the alarm clock that signals when to get out of bed every morning. Even though alarms are useful, not everyone enjoys hearing them.

The Versatile Modern Watch

Every busy modern person needs a watch. Not only do watches tell the time, but the latest versions can do a great many other things. For example, many watches show the exact month and date. But that is not all. You can find watches that tell the temperature, glow in the dark, and tell the time of other time zones. Some watches have a calculator. Others have a stopwatch. That is, they will measure how much time it takes to do something. A great addition is the watch that has an alarm signal. Businesspeople set the alarm to ring when they need to make an important call, end a meeting, or wake up while traveling. In our time-conscious world, a watch is too convenient and necessary to be without.

TOPIC 2: "How is jewelry today different from jewelry worn in ancient times?"

History of Jewelry

No one really knows when the first jewelry was made. Probably the first simple pieces of jewelry were worn as a protection of the gods to keep the wearer safe from harm. These were made of shells, precious stones, or other hard materials like teeth or glass. Later on, jewelry was worn to show position or wealth. Evidence from ancient burial sites shows that the most important people wore the most jewelry. They wore rings, earrings, necklaces, and arm-, leg-, and headbands. By the time of recorded history, most jewelry was formed from precious metals like gold and silver. The early Egyptians liked to use blue and red stones in their jewelry, while the early Italians preferred decorated gold without added gemstones. All jewelry was made by hand, and even today, the best jewelry is made by skilled artisans.

Now, a lot of jewelry is made by machine. This type is called costume jewelry. It is inexpensive because it is often made from a combination of plastic and metal. Styles of jewelry have changed over the years just as styles of clothes have. Nevertheless, since most people like to wear jewelry, it will probably never go out of fashion.

Gemstone Superstitions

There have been many superstitions about gemstones even though people love them for their brilliance and beauty. These superstitions were not all bad because certain stones were supposed to make those who wore them strong, wise, or protected from fire and lightning. The idea of birthstones came from these common superstitions. People believed that a person's future was influenced by the qualities of the gemstone of his or her birth month. For example, rubies were supposed to bring wealth and happiness, emeralds could tell the future, and diamonds could protect from danger. Birthstones popular today are: garnet (January), amethyst (February), aquamarine (March), diamond (April), emerald (May), pearl (June), ruby (July), peridot (August), sapphire (September), opal (October), topaz (November), and turquoise (December). Not many people believe the superstitions anymore, but most people enjoy wearing the stones of their birth month because they are beautiful and lasting.

Using Information from Printed Sources

In a research paper you will use thoughts, ideas, and facts from other authors to explain your topic. This borrowed information is written within the paper in three ways: paraphrase, summary, and quotation. To paraphrase means to use your own words to write someone else's idea without changing the meaning. To summarize means to write the main idea or ideas of a paragraph, a section, or an article. To quote means to use someone else's exact words. A paraphrase, a summary, and a quotation each require a citation. Citations will be presented in Chapter 17.

PART 1 *Paraphrasing*

When you paraphrase, you use your own words to tell what someone else said or wrote without changing the original meaning or leaving out details.

You paraphrase by:

- using synonyms
- expressing the ideas in your own sentences

A paraphrase:

- is about as long as the original information
- contains all the details of the original

Example:

Original text: The citizens of Ashton are complaining loudly about the problems and inefficiency of the sanitation system, because Friday the sanitation crew removed approximately half the refuse on Center Street, and it wasn't until Saturday that they returned and removed that which remained.

Paraphrase: Garbage removal for the people of Ashton has been a problem. They are unhappy about the way the garbage collectors have done their job. For example, only half of the garbage was removed on Friday. They finally came back on Saturday to take the rest of it away.

In this example, the writer changed the word order and made these word changes:

"citizens of Ashton" ➔ people of Ashton

"complaining loudly" ➔ unhappy

"sanitation system"   ➔ garbage removal

"sanitation crew"   ➔ garbage collectors

What other changes do you see?

1. _____

2. _____

3. _____

PRACTICE 1

Paraphrasing

▼ Read the following paragraph with a classmate.

▼ Explain the paragraph to a classmate in your own words.

▼ Write down what you said.

▼ If you have included all the information, and your paragraph looks different from the original, you have written a good paraphrase.

Paragraph 1

   Recycling can be made easy. Call your local government office and find out what can be recycled in the area and how that material will be taken to the recycling businesses. Many cities have curbside collection services for glass, newspaper, and aluminum.

_____

_____

_____

Paragraph 2

Garbage dumps in the United States are filling up fast. For this reason, many industries must pay the local governments a fee to use the dump. As a consequence, some industries are shipping the garbage out to sea and dumping it there. The problem is that often this garbage is washed up on beaches and creates an ugly, unhealthy situation.

_____

_____

_____

Paragraph 3

Because "10 percent of air pollution comes from the nation's 89 million lawn mowers, garden tractors, chain saws, and other gas-powered garden equipment," the Environmental Protection Agency is thinking about putting emission standards on these machines, just as it does on automobiles. This will cause an extra financial burden on the citizens, but it might help to clean up the air in places where there is a high concentration of people.

(Courtesy of The Daily Universe)

_____

_____

_____

_____

_____

_____

PART 2 *Summarizing Parts of Articles*

When you summarize, you put the writer's main ideas into your own words.

You summarize:

- an entire article

- part of an article

- one paragraph

You want to summarize to:

- shorten a large amount of material

- leave out unnecessary details

- quickly state the most important ideas or facts

- make sure that the paper is in your own words

In academic writing, a summary of the independent ideas of a specific writer must have a reference to that writer.

Read the original report about garbage collection in Ashton again. Then read the following summaries.

Original text

The citizens of Ashton are complaining loudly about the problems and inefficiency of the sanitation system, because Friday the sanitation crew removed approximately half the refuse on Center Street, and it wasn't until Saturday that they returned and removed that which remained.

Summary 1

The garbage collection crew in Ashton is not working efficiently, and the people who live there are unhappy about it (Mahoney, 1993).

Summary 2

Mahoney said that the garbage collection crew in Ashton is not doing the job efficiently, and the people who live there are unhappy about it (1993).

Notice that 1 and 2 have different information in the parentheses. Do you know why?

PRACTICE 2

Summarizing Paragraphs

▼ Read these paragraphs again.

▼ Write a summary of each one.

Paragraph 1

Recycling can be made easy. All you have to do is to call your local government office and find out what can be recycled in the area and how that material will be taken to the recycling businesses. Many cities have collection services for glass, newspaper, and aluminum.

_____

_____

_____

Paragraph 2

Garbage dumps in the United States are filling up fast. For this reason, many industries must pay the local governments a fee to use the dump. As a consequence, some industries are shipping the garbage out to sea and dumping it there. The problem is that often this garbage is washed up on beaches and creates an ugly, unhealthy situation.

_____

_____

_____

_____

Paragraph 3

Because "10 percent of air pollution comes from the nation's 89 million lawn mowers, garden tractors, chain saws, and other gas-powered garden equipment," the Environmental Protection Agency is thinking about putting emission standards on these machines, just as it does on automobiles. This will cause an extra financial burden on the citizens, but it might help to clean up the air in places where there is a high concentration of people.

(Courtesy of The Daily Universe)

_____

_____

_____

_____

PRACTICE 3

Paraphrasing and Summarizing Paragraphs

Follow these steps:

1. Find a paragraph in a newspaper or magazine.

2. In your notebook, write down the name of the newspaper or magazine, the date it was published, the author of the article (if there is one), and the page number.

3. Copy the paragraph into your notebook.

4. Write a paraphrase of the paragraph.

5. Write a summary of the paragraph.

6. Have a classmate evaluate your paraphrase and summary.

PART 3 *Quotations*

When you quote, you use the author's exact words in your paper.

You quote because the author:

● wrote clear and exact words that you think are valuable

● is an authority you trust and you want to use his or her authority to explain your idea or opinion

● wrote unique words that will add interest

You will use more summaries and paraphrases and fewer quotations in an academic research paper.

1. For short quotations (fewer than 40 words):

● put quotation marks around the exact words you take from another author

● write the quotation within the paragraph

Examples:

1. "Scientists miscalculated the amount of radiation released when the Chernobyl nuclear reactor disaster occurred" (Adam, 1994, p. 5).

2. Jenson stated, "Nuclear reactors require strict safety codes" (1993, p. 64).

3. For long quotations (40 or more words):

    - Do not use quotation marks. Instead, indent all lines five spaces from the left margin.

    - Double space the quoted lines.

    - Put the period at the end of the quotation.

    - Then put the citation at the end of the sentence.

    - Use very few long quotations in a paper.

Example:

> Since the environment seems to be in need of protecting, one of the key ways is to recycle anything that can be used again. This will prevent the rapid decline of our nation's natural resources. To support this claim, Jones said,
>
>> Recycled materials can be substituted for virgin materials (ones that come directly from the earth) and would reduce such problems as strip-mining and deforestation. Production of virgin materials also uses more fossil fuels and other resources which could be saved by recycling. (1993, p. 6)
>
> *(Courtesy of* The Daily Universe)

PRACTICE 4

Writing Quotations

▼ Read the following newspaper article about recycling.

▼ Find two interesting facts to quote, one short and one long.

▼ Write the quotations on the lines at the end of the article.

▼ Be sure that you have the correct punctuation.

Source: Jones, J. (Mar. 31, 1993). Utah down in dumps with recycling efforts. The Daily Universe, p. 6.

Utah Down in the Dumps with Recycling Efforts

Utah's state government must take an active part in encouraging people to preserve the environment. One of the best ways everyone can become involved is through recycling. Voluntary action by the people of Utah is currently very low, and the state must take some form of action in increasing the amount of recycling done by citizens.

What are the merits of recycling? Right now only 13 percent of all garbage is recycled. Most of the garbage ends up in overflowing landfills that contaminate underground water. The rest is burned in high-temperature furnaces that send toxic pollutants into the air. In contrast, recycling is a safer, less costly solution to the problem of waste disposal. Recycling reduces the amount of solid waste taken to landfills and incinerators and thereby decreases the amount of water and air pollution.

One of the most important reasons for recycling is to preserve natural resources. Recycled materials can be substituted for natural materials (ones that come directly from the earth) and would reduce such problems as strip-mining and deforestation. Production of natural materials also uses more fossil fuels and other resources that could be saved by recycling.

Contrary to popular belief, recycling also saves governments and citizens money. For example, businesses and individuals can reduce their waste disposal costs by more than 70 percent by using a recycling program. Also, individuals or communities receive money from selling recyclables to recycling companies. So businesses are not only saving money, they are earning money as well.

Furthermore, production using recycled materials is usually cheaper for a company and reduces the cost of pollution control. In addition, the recycling industry provides employment for hundreds of thousands of people.

In spite of all these benefits, however, recycling in Utah is quite limited. In Provo and Orem, residents must pay a $3.00 monthly charge for pickup of recyclable materials limited only to newspapers, magazines, cardboard, aluminum, and tin. Unfortunately, the enrollment in this program is also small—2,000 households. In Salt Lake County, none of the communities has a curbside recycling plan. Salt Lake City, the major city in the county, will begin one in the near future.

Still, the state of Utah is six years behind many other states in their recycling programs and must put forth a greater effort to promote recycling. The state must become environmentally responsible. The state government must act quickly to set recycling goals and implement a recycling program.

(Courtesy of The Daily Universe)

Short quotation:

_____

_____

Long quotation:

_____

_____

_____

_____

When doing a research paper, note cards help you keep track of two important types of information:

- the sources in which you find information
- the information that you want to use

There are two kinds of cards:

- bibliography cards
- note cards

PART 4 *Bibliography Cards*

Bibliography cards list the source of the information you used and show where all the borrowed information came from. The information on these cards will be used in your reference list.

Examples:

Book

Type: **Book**
Title: **Poaching: A Curse!**
Author: **Charles Adair**
Year published: **1990**
Publisher: **Diamante Press**
Where published: **Madrid**

Periodical

Type: **Magazine**
Name of Periodical: **Animal News**
Title of Article: **Apes**
Author: **John Longhurst**
Volume and number: **none**
Date: **Jan. 2, 1989**
Pages: **44–47**

PART 5 *Note Cards*

Note cards are usually 3 × 5 or 5 × 7 cards on which you have written information that answers your research question. Because this information is from other writers, you show in your paper where the information came from. Each card should have the following information:

1. Last name of author and year the information was published.
2. Page number(s) on which the information is found.
3. Key word or signal word that tells the main idea of the information.
4. The information—a quotation, paraphrase, or summary.
5. The way you recorded the information (Q, P, or S).

Examples:

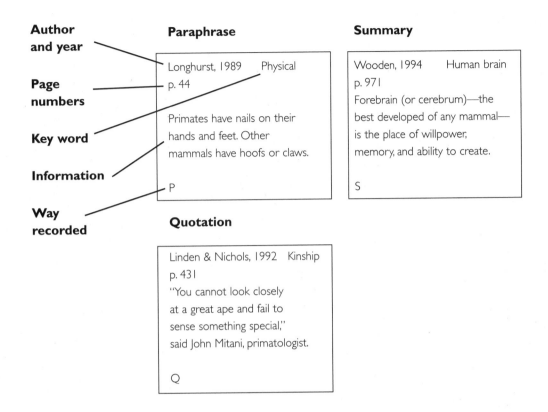

Author and year

Page numbers

Key word

Information

Way recorded

Paraphrase

Longhurst, 1989   Physical
p. 44

Primates have nails on their
hands and feet. Other
mammals have hoofs or claws.

P

Summary

Wooden, 1994   Human brain
p. 971
Forebrain (or cerebrum)—the
best developed of any mammal—
is the place of willpower,
memory, and ability to create.

S

Quotation

Linden & Nichols, 1992   Kinship
p. 431
"You cannot look closely
at a great ape and fail to
sense something special,"
said John Mitani, primatologist.

Q

Remember:

- Summary and paraphrase notes are in your own words.
- Quotations are the exact words of the author.

P R A C T I C E 5

*Writing Key Words on
Note Cards*

The key word on a note card will help you organize all the "borrowed" information. It also quickly reminds you what information is on the card.

Here are some more note cards on the topic of primates. Read each note card and write a key word in the upper right hand corner. You might have to use 2–3 words to tell what the main idea of the card is.

1.
| Linden & Nichols, 1992 _____ |
| p. 16 |
| Gibbons have long fingers and toes that are curved to help them hold onto branches as they swing through trees. |
| P |

2.
| Linden & Nichols, 1992 _____ |
| p. 16 |
| Most of the time apes climb through trees or walk on the ground on all fours. Of all the species, gibbons spend the most time walking on two legs. |
| S |

3.
| Linden & Nichols, 1992 _____ |
| p. 16 |
| Because of the close genetic similarities between chimpanzees and humans, chimps are used in human research. |
| P |

4.
| Linden & Nichols, 1992 _____ |
| p. 44 |
| "Like all ape species, gorilla females ovulate about once a month and usually bear one infant at a time." |
| Q |

5.
| Linden & Nichols, 1992 _____ |
| p. 5 |
| Gorilla babies are very dependent. They may not leave their mother's arms until they are three months old. |
| P |

6.
| Linden & Nichols, 1992 _____ |
| p. 12, 13 |
| Since Jane Goodall's observation in 1960, " . . . Every chimp group studied has proven to use tools." |
| Q |

PART 6 *From Note Cards to Planning Outline*

After you finish taking notes and begin to put them in groups, a planning outline will begin to form in your mind. You'll start to see where each piece of information will go in your outline.

Look at this simple illustration of where information might fit in an outline.

Topic: Compare humans to primates

Research Question: How are people and primates different?

Thesis Statement: Human intelligence makes people different from any other primates.

Planning Outline

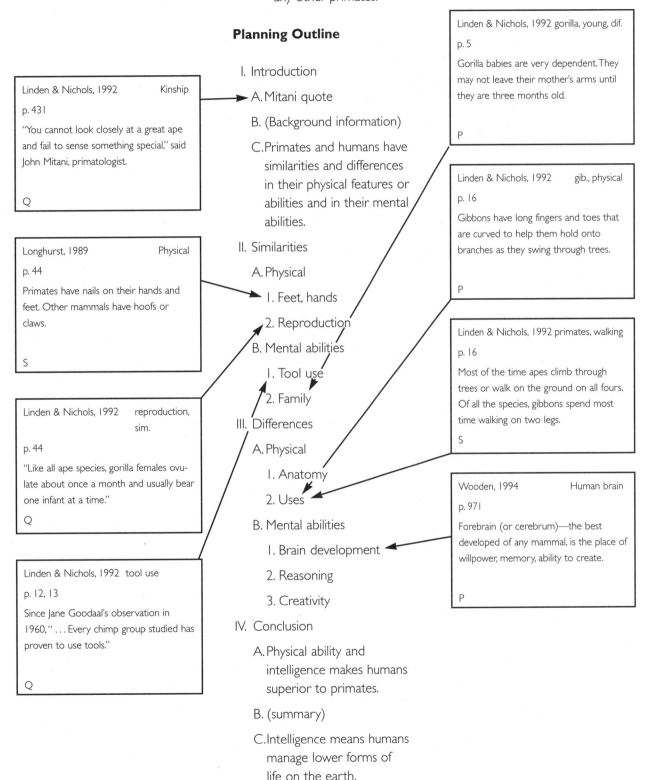

Linden & Nichols, 1992   Kinship

p. 431

"You cannot look closely at a great ape and fail to sense something special," said John Mitani, primatologist.

Q

Longhurst, 1989   Physical

p. 44

Primates have nails on their hands and feet. Other mammals have hoofs or claws.

S

Linden & Nichols, 1992   reproduction, sim.

p. 44

"Like all ape species, gorilla females ovulate about once a month and usually bear one infant at a time."

Q

Linden & Nichols, 1992 tool use

p. 12, 13

Since Jane Goodall's observation in 1960, "... Every chimp group studied has proven to use tools."

Q

Linden & Nichols, 1992 gorilla, young, dif.

p. 5

Gorilla babies are very dependent. They may not leave their mother's arms until they are three months old.

P

Linden & Nichols, 1992   gib., physical

p. 16

Gibbons have long fingers and toes that are curved to help them hold onto branches as they swing through trees.

P

Linden & Nichols, 1992 primates, walking

p. 16

Most of the time apes climb through trees or walk on the ground on all fours. Of all the species, gibbons spend most time walking on two legs.

S

Wooden, 1994   Human brain

p. 971

Forebrain (or cerebrum)—the best developed of any mammal, is the place of willpower, memory, ability to create.

P

I. Introduction

  A. Mitani quote

  B. (Background information)

  C. Primates and humans have similarities and differences in their physical features or abilities and in their mental abilities.

II. Similarities

  A. Physical

    1. Feet, hands

    2. Reproduction

  B. Mental abilities

    1. Tool use

    2. Family

III. Differences

  A. Physical

    1. Anatomy

    2. Uses

  B. Mental abilities

    1. Brain development

    2. Reasoning

    3. Creativity

IV. Conclusion

  A. Physical ability and intelligence makes humans superior to primates.

  B. (summary)

  C. Intelligence means humans manage lower forms of life on the earth.

CHAPTER 16

Academic Honesty

INTRODUCTION

Plagiarize comes from a Latin word meaning "to kidnap," which means to take a person by force or against his or her will. In English, the words *plagiarize, plagiarism,* and *plagiarizing* mean to take some words or ideas from someone else and use them as if they were your own. This is academic dishonesty or cheating.

Since universities and colleges expect students to do their own work, students can be asked to leave a university if they are cheating, being dishonest, or plagiarizing. To avoid serious problems:

- do not copy words from others

- do not copy ideas from others

- do not have someone else do your work

Here are statements about plagiarism from some universities:

> **Rice University, Houston, Texas:** "The following pledge shall be signed at the end of all final examinations, hour quizzes, and other important projects on which the pledge is required by the instructor: On my honor, I have neither given nor received any aid on this (examination, quiz, or paper)."

> **University of Pennsylvania, Philadelphia, Pa.:** "Any work that a student undertakes as a part of the progress toward a degree or certification must be the student's own, unless the relevant instructor specifies otherwise."

> **Yale University, New Haven, Conn.:** "The provisions against cheating must be understood to include all forms of misrepresentation in academic work, including: The submission of the same paper in more than one course without explicit authorization of the appropriate instructors; Cheating on tests, examinations, problem sets, or any other exercise; Any form of plagiarism, especially failure to acknow-

ledge ideas or language taken from others, and the submission of work prepared by another person; Submission of a scientific research report that misrepresents in any way the work actually done."

(Cited in The Daily Universe)

P A R T 1 *Avoiding Plagiarism*

A paper has information from three sources:

- your own ideas and observations
- general information you can find in many places
- specific information, phrases, and ideas that you get from others

When you include information you obtained through research, you will need two things in order to avoid plagiarism.

1. *A citation* is a short reference given within your paper that shows the reader who wrote it and where it came from. The citation is written in parentheses. An APA citation usually looks like this: (Brown, 1993).

2. *A reference list* is a complete alphabetical list of all the sources you used. Each type of source (magazine, journal, newspaper, book) will have a different form.

P A R T 2 *A Citation*

A citation is:

- a bibliographic abbreviation to help the reader find the source of the information on the reference list
- used every time you use borrowed information that you recorded on a note card (summary, paraphrase, quotation)
- written inside parentheses ( ) at the end of the borrowed information in your paper

PART 3   *From Bibliographic Information to Note Card to Citation*

Look at the following example of how the bibliographic information you write on the card will help you write a correct citation.

Bibliographic information

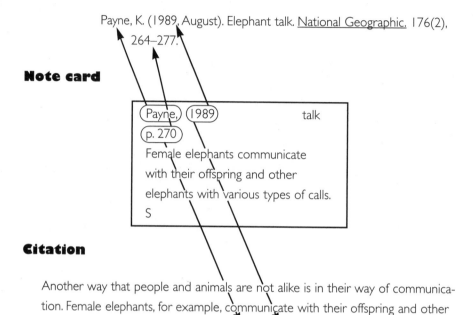

Payne, K. (1989, August). Elephant talk. <u>National Geographic.</u> 176(2), 264–277.

Note card

Payne, 1989   talk
p. 270
Female elephants communicate
with their offspring and other
elephants with various types of calls.
S

Citation

Another way that people and animals are not alike is in their way of communication. Female elephants, for example, communicate with their offspring and other elephants with various types of calls (Payne, 1989).

Examples of Correct Citations

Here is some information from the article on apes in "People and Apes: A Comparison" written by Mae, C., 1994, on page 12 in *Animal News*. This information might be used in comparing families of animals and humans.

Original information

Chimpanzees live in a large, loosely organized group that breaks into smaller groups in which the individuals are constantly changing. *Family* groups of other species, such as the bonobos, consist of older dominant females with only their young males or babies.

If you wish to use the information, it might look like one of these in your paper:

Paraphrase:

The families of chimps are casually arranged into smaller groups that always change. The bonobos' families are ruled by older females who live with only the young male children or babies (Mae, 1994).

Summary:

Some primates have families that are constantly changing or are totally dominated by an older female (Mae, 1994).

Quotation:

Bonobos' family groups "consist of older dominant females with only their young males or babies" (Mae, 1994, p. 12).

As a class, discuss the answers to these questions:

1. What are the differences in each of the citations above?
2. What is the difference in punctuation in each citation?

Examples of Plagiarism

Below are examples of plagiarized information from the paragraph about chimpanzees. Compare each one with the original above.

Plagiarism 1

Chimpanzees live in big families which are loosely organized.

Problems:

- It follows the same word order as the original.
- "loosely organized" are the exact words of the original.
- There is no citation.

Plagiarism 2

Groups of other species, such as the bonobos, consist of older dominant females.

Problems:

- These are the exact words of the original, so quotation marks are needed.
- There is no citation indicating the author, year, and page number.

> **Remember, if you do not use a citation when you use specific information, phrases, or ideas from other writers, you are plagiarizing.**

PRACTICE 1

Matching Note Cards
to Citations

▼ Read the information on the note cards below.

▼ Read the short essay below, which uses the information on the cards.

▼ Write the number of the card on the line near the citation in the essay.

1.

Angus et al.1990	Lifestyle
p. 67	

Laws of nature=kill others, even brothers or weaker animals. Compete to survive. Strongest win.

S

2.

"Best Sellers"1993	Instinct
p. B2	

Women love books about pregnancy and caring for babies. They sell well at all bookstores.

S

3.

Morgan 1993	Intelligence
p. 57	

"Only a few animals have even close to the same brain-power as the human brain and these animals are all primates."

Q

4.

Shower & Goodson1991	Instinct
p. 25	

Cats and other animals begin licking their young soon after birth. This is thought to bond the mother to the baby.

P

5.

Morgan 1993	Instinct
p. 59	

Human beings have to learn things other animals know by instinct.

P

6.

Watkins 1989	Lifestyle
p. 6	

Bears live alone. They only come together to mate.

P

Animals and Humans

Animals cannot be considered equal to human beings because they do not have the same intelligence. Pigs are quite intelligent and so are dolphins, but according to Morgan (1993), "Only a few animals have even close to the same brain-power as the human brain and these animals are all primates" (p. 57).

There are physical acts that animals share with people, but animals perform these acts instinctively; whereas, human beings normally need to learn them (p. 59). One instance of this is the way animals care for their young. A mother cat instinctively will begin licking the baby kittens as soon

_____ as they are born (Shower & Goodson, 1991). The human mother has fewer instincts about her baby and often needs to turn to others, such as her own mother, a friend, or a neighbor to learn how to care for a baby. Some mothers are so anxious that they spend their entire pregnancy reading books on the subject of caring for infants. Therefore, sales of books on pregnancy and care of children are always popular in urban _____ bookstores ("Best Sellers," 1993).

_____ Other differences between animals and people are in social organization. People build houses and live in family groups, tribes, villages, towns, or larger cities. Watkins (1989) explains, however, that many animals, such as bears, never live in groups, but only contact other animals of the same kind to mate. Another difference is that animals live by the laws of nature, often killing other smaller animals for food. They have no feelings about killing even weaker animals of their own kind because in the world of nature, there is constant competition between animals, and only the _____ strongest tend to survive (Angus et al., 1990). On the other hand, human beings apply their intelligence to create working societies and laws to prevent the act of killing other people.

PART 4 *Writing Citations in APA Style*

The basic citation gives the author and the date of the source of your information. In this way, the reader can quickly find that source in your reference list.

1. Standard Citations

▼ Read these examples of different types of citations.

▼ Do not memorize them.

▼ Refer to them as you write your paper.

A. Summary or Paraphrase (Give Author and Date Only.)

Example 1:

The standard citation uses only the last name of the author and the year of publication in parentheses. There is a comma between the author and the year.

An expert claimed that all hawks have eggs that are damaged by the insecticide DDT **(Jones, 1992).** This means that the shells of the eggs will break when the mother sits on the nest. If Jones is correct, no baby hawks will be born to replace the adults that die.

Example 2:

If the author is already named in your own sentence, write the year in the parentheses just after the author's name.

> **Jones (1992)** claimed that all hawks have eggs that are damaged by the insecticide DDT. This means that the shells of the eggs will break when the mother sits on the nest. If Jones is correct, no baby hawks will be born to replace the adults that die.

Example 3:

If no author is given, use the first words of the title in quotation marks.

> The largest source of iron in our diet should be grains. Too many people think that the only source of iron is red meat (**"Eating Wise,"** 1993).

Example 4:

If the work has two authors, always give both authors and use **&** between the authors' names in the citation. Use **and** if the authors are mentioned in your own sentence.

> Surveys have shown that women at any age are not absorbing enough calcium during their lifetimes to offset osteoporosis. Supplements of this mineral are vital at any age (**Arbourn & Hall, 1979**).

Example 5:

If the citation has three to five authors, the first citation in the paper lists all the authors. Any additional citations have only the first author's name with **et al.** after the name.

> Most problems with excess weight come from eating too many fatty foods or foods with hidden fat, not an excess of sugar. The problem is that usually whatever is sweet is surrounded by fatty substances as well (**Nielsen, Arbourn, Leddell, & Meyers, 1994**).
>
> Because of the fight against sugary food, many manufacturers have now turned to an increased amount of corn syrup in their products, claiming that the food is "naturally" sweetened (**Nielsen et al., 1994**).

Note: A citation with **more than five authors** is written with the first author and **et al.** to represent all the other authors.

B. Quotations
(Give author, date,
and page numbers.)

Example 6:

The citation is placed just after the quotation marks even if the quotation is in the middle of the sentence.

> "The chemicals found in DDT weaken the shells of hawks' eggs to the point that the female cannot sit on them without breaking them" (Jones, 1992, p. 39), so this is causing great concern among environmentalists.

Example 7:

If the author is named before the quotation in your own sentence, write the year in parentheses after the author's name and the page number in parentheses at the end of the quotation. End with a period after the last parenthesis.

> **Jones (1992)** said, "The chemicals found in DDT weaken the shells of hawks' eggs to the point that the female cannot sit on them without breaking them" **(p. 39)**.

Example 8:

When more than one author is quoted, the citation is placed immediately after the information from each author.

> When looking at diet needs, **Jensen** stated, "Avoid all fat. It is bad for your body" **(1989, p. 43)**, but **Meldrum** has a moderate view, "Everyone needs some fat in their diet" **(1990, p. 124)**.

Example 9:

If a quotation citation has the same author as your last citation but has a different page number, place the new page number in the citation after the information.

> **Arbourn (1991)** stated, "Studies have shown that broccoli and cauliflower have the necessary natural substances to prevent cancer" (p. 89). He further said, "Most all vegetables have good antioxidant and anticancer capabilities, and to eat seven servings of vegetables a day is better than swallowing multivitamin and mineral tablets" **(p. 90)**.

Example 10:

When you want to use words an author has quoted from someone else, use single quote marks (' ') around the original quotation.

> **Carter (1989) quoted Dr. Henry Eliason,** 'No matter which road of life they travel, they will all end up at the same place' (p. 7) when Carter pointed out that death is at the end of every life.

PART 5 *Preparing Your Reader for Citations*

As you use borrowed information in your paper, you should prepare your reader for the information. In all the examples above, you read phrases such as these.

These phrases introduced summaries and paraphrases:

An expert claimed that . . .	Surveys have shown that . . .
Jones said that . . .	Carter pointed out that . . .

These phrases introduced quotations:

Jones said, ". . .	Carter quoted Dr. Henry Eliason, ". . .
Jensen stated, ". . .	He further said, ". . .

Here are some words and phrases that are used to prepare readers for borrowed information. As you write your paper, try to use a variety of these introductory words. However, be sure you understand the meaning of the word before you use it. Be sure to use either present or past tense consistently to introduce cited information.

say/said	analyze	reveal	explain
report	comment	state	mention
add	confirm	note	find
write	describe	observe	claim
suggest	record	believe	argue
remark	admits	offer	conclude
according to . . .	In the opinion of . . .	. . . points out that . . .	
In the words/writing of . . .		As _____ has said, . . .	

PRACTICE 2

Recognizing Citations

▼ Match the type of citation in each exercise to one of the examples on pages 00–00.

▼ Write the example letter on the blank next to the citation.

Exercise 1

Amazing Mammals: Dolphins

Dolphins, generally, are really rather noisy. "...with their blow holes they
1. _____ squeak, quack, squawk, creak, and whistle" (McGowen, 1980, p. 40).

Larger dolphins are called the bottle-nosed dolphin. McGowen (1980)
2. _____ says, "A full-grown adult may be 11 to 12 feet long" (p. 36).

The Amazon River dolphin is quite different from other dolphins. When it
is young, it has a pink underside and it is gray on top. When it grows to an
adult, it is pink all over. It also has very small eyes and hair on its beak
3. _____ (Patent, 1987).

(Javier Cerdio—Mexico)

Exercise 2

Water Pollution

Microbiological contaminants may be found in drinking water. Some of
these include "Giardia, Cryptosporidium, Yersinia enterolitica, Leginella, and
1. _____ several viruses" (Sly, 1991, p. 340).

2. _____ Also iron bacteria combine with iron to contaminate water ("Sublette,"
3. _____ 1992). Ciesielski (1991) suggested that there is a stronger potential source
of water contamination in rural areas. In fact, three kinds of intestinal para-
sites were recently found in random samples of water in migrant labor
camps. Furthermore, "In Florida, an echovirus was isolated from water
samples in a migrant camp during an outbreak of gastrointestinal illness"
4. _____ (p. 763).

A common disinfectant is chlorine and its compounds. Chlorine is commonly used to purify drinking water in many cities of America. People
object to the odor but "the chlorine added to drinking water in the U.S.
has produced dramatic reductions in water-borne diseases such as typhoid
5. _____ fever" (Fackelman, 1992, p. 23). However, Morris and Audet (1992) have
6. _____ determined that there is an association between drinking chlorinated
water and cancer, particularly bladder and rectal cancer.

7. _____ In fact, Fackelman (1992) claims, "People who drink chlorinated water run a 21 percent greater risk of bladder cancer and a 38 percent greater risk of rectal cancer than people who drink water with little or no chlorine"

8. _____ (p. 23). Recently, a new compound of chlorine and ammonia has become widespread because it has less risk. Although this method is safer than the

9. _____ others, it is not completely safe (Fackelman, 1992).

(Monika Tobolewski—Poland)

P A R T 6 *References for Periodicals and Books, APA Style*

The following list reviews the references for periodicals and adds references for books.

1. Professional journal article

Form:

Author's last name, Initials. (year). Title of article. Name of the Journal, Vol. #, page numbers.

Example:

Paivio, A. (1975). Perceptual comparisons through the mind's eye. Memory & Cognition, 3, 635–647.

2. Magazine article

Form:

Author's last name, Initial/s. (year, month day). Title of article, Name of Magazine, page numbers.

Example:

Johnson, J. (1991, June 13). Is America becoming dishonest? Men and Women Today, pp. 70–76.

3. Newspaper article

Form:

Author's last name, Initials. (year, month day). Title of article. Name of Newspaper, page number.

Example:

O'Leary, K. (1992, February 14). Ethical decisions a part of everyday existence, speaker tells students. <u>The Daily Universe</u>, p. 4.

4. Newspaper article, no author

Form:

Title of article. (year, month day). <u>Name of newspaper</u>, page number.

Example:

Bush outlines aid to former republics. (1992, April 2). <u>Langley Gazette</u>, p. B1

5. Book with one author

Form:

Author's last name, Initials. (year). <u>Title of book</u>. Location: Publisher.

Example:

Burley, D. (1994). <u>Holidays in France</u>. Paris: Furtado Books, Inc.

6. Book without author, with editors

Form:

Names of editors, (Eds.). (year). <u>Title of book</u>. Location: Publisher.

Example:

Newton, F., & Francum, P. (Eds.). (1989). <u>Africa, a land of plenty</u>. New York: York Associates.

7. Book without author or editor

Form:

<u>Title of book</u>. (year). Location: Publisher.

Example:

<u>Helps for freshmen</u>. (1992). Salt Lake City, UT: University Press.

8. Book with two to four authors

Form:

Name of author 1, Initial(s), Name of author 2, Initial(s), & Name of author 3,
   Initial(s). (year). <u>Title of book</u>. Location: Publisher.

Example:

Gilly, M., Johnson, D., O'Dell, E., & Graham, R. (1986). <u>American customs reviewed</u>.
   Chicago: Molland Publishers.

PRACTICE 3

*Identifying Citations
and References*

Do the following exercises as you examine parts of other students' comparison-and-contrast research papers. You will look at the reference list and the citations below it.

▼ Read the sources in the reference list.

▼ Tell if the reference is a **book, periodical,** or **other.** Write one of the words in the blank.

▼ Circle all the citations in the paragraphs.

▼ Identify the source of each citation. Write the numbers of the references next to each paragraph.

Exercise 1

Designers: Ralph Lauren and Calvin Klein

References

1. __Book__   <u>Fairchild's who's who in fashion</u>. (1975). Calvin Klein. Fairchild
      Publications, Inc.

2. _____ <u>Fairchild's who's who in fashion</u>. (1988). Ralph Lauren. Fairchild
      Publications, Inc.

3. _____ Gross, M. (1988, August 8). The latest Calvin. <u>New York</u>. pp. 20–29.

4. _____ Trachtenberg, J. (1988). <u>Ralph Lauren, the man behind the mystique</u>.
      Boston: Little, Brown and Company.

A. <u>3, 4</u> Both Trachtenberg (1988) and Gross (1988) say that Lauren and Klein grew up in the Bronx in New York. Lauren was born on October 14, _____ 1939 (Trachtenberg, 1988) and Klein was born on November 19, 1942 _____ (Gross, 1988).

B. _____ Lauren started his own business in 1967 and established the famous "Polo" brand in 1968 without any prior training in design (<u>Fairchild's Who's Who in Fashion</u>, 1975). Klein worked five years at a large firm as an apprentice and designer, and then he established Calvin Klein Limited in _____ 1968 (<u>Fairchild's Who's Who</u>, 1988).

C. _____ Both Klein and Lauren wanted their fragrances (perfumes) to be like European fragrances. Famous European designers had been making their own fragrances for many years and were very successful. "... Chanel put her name on Chanel No. 5 in the early 1920s. Jeanne Lanvin introduced My Sin in 1925. Jean Patou launched Joy in 1930, and Christian Dior pre-_____ sented Miss Dior in 1947" (Trachtenberg, 1988, p. 163).

(Matsuoka Yuko—Japan)

Exercise 2

Roses and Chrysanthemums

References

1. _____ Burke, K. (1993). <u>All about the roses</u>. California: Ortho Books.

2. _____ Hessayon, D. (1991). <u>The new house plant expert</u>. London: PBI Publications.

3. _____ Shuling, Z. (1981). <u>Chinese chrysanthemums</u>. Beijing: Shaohua Publishing House.

A. _____ Another similarity is the origin of the two flowers. The Chinese were the first to cultivate roses (Burke, 1993). Shuling (1981) says that the chrysanthemum also is native to China, and the Chinese love this flower not only for its beauty, but also for other characteristics as well.

B. _____ Confucius wrote about roses in the Imperial Gardens. Moreover, the ancient Greeks cultivated roses especially for making medicines and perfumes. The Roman Empire imported roses from Egypt and planted them in monastery gardens. In England during the 15th century, two royal families who were fighting over the throne took white and red roses as their respective symbols, so the war was called "the War of the Roses." Since _____ that time roses have been the symbol of English royalty (Burke, 1993).

C.   In contrast, "the chrysanthemum is a typical representative of the family _____ *Compositae*" (Shuling, 1981, p. 61). According to Hessayon (1991) there are only two types of chrysanthemums. The first one can be grown in a greenhouse. It produces a single flower in the summer and autumn which can be white, orange, yellow, pink, or red. The second one generally flowers in the summer and has a yellow center that is surrounded by white, yellow, or pink petals.

(Mario Diaz—Guatemala)

> **Complete your paper and make sure that you have a citation for all borrowed information and a reference for each source of information. Your rough draft is now ready for an evaluation.**

PART 7   *Peer Evaluation: Comparison-and-Contrast Research Paper*

▼ Put an *S* (Satisfactory) or a *U* (Unsatisfactory) in the blank in front of each item.

▼ Write the total number of *S*'s and *U*'s at the top.

Name of writer _____   Total *S*'s _____

Name of evaluator_____   Total *U*'s_____

Date_____

Title page and outline

_____   1. Title page is in the correct form.

_____   2. utline page has the title <u>Outline</u>.

_____   3. Outline uses the correct numbers and letters.

_____   4. Outline has logical categories.

_____   5. Outline is in the student's own words.

Introduction of the paper

_____   6. The introduction has a hook.

_____   7. Background information defines, explains, or gives facts that stay with the topic.

_____   8. There is a clear thesis statement. (<u>Underline</u> what you think is the thesis statement.)

Body of paper

_____   9. Paper is at least three typed pages (six pages handwritten).

_____   10. Paper has at least five citations.

_____   11. Paper has one quotation.

_____   12. Citations are done correctly. (Page numbers given in all citations in this draft.)

_____   13. Cited information adds interest to the paper.

_____ 14. New paragraphs are indented.

_____ 15. Each paragraph in the body of the paper has a topic sentence.

_____ 16. Order of the paper matches the order of the outline.

Conclusion of the paper

_____ 17. Conclusion restates the ideas of the thesis statement.

_____ 18. Conclusion summarizes the body of the paper.

_____ 19. Conclusion has a good final sentence.

Reference list

_____ 20. Reference list has the title *References*.

_____ 21. Reference list has at least two sources listed in alphabetical order.

_____ 22. Sources are in correct APA style.

Note cards

_____ 23. Notes are mostly paraphrases or summaries.

_____ 24. Notes are in correct form.

Optional for the first draft

_____ 25. The paper is in a three-hole pocket folder with student's name on the cover.

_____ 26. The paper is in the correct order: title page, outline, paper, bibliography.

_____ 27. In the pocket of the folder or in a large envelope are these items: note cards, copies of articles, student evaluation sheet.

Tell the writer what you liked about this paper.

_____

_____

Give the writer a few suggestions to improve the paper.

_____

_____

_____

**Write your second draft by making the necessary revisions that were suggested.
Hand it in for editing corrections.**

Write your third draft by making the grammar, spelling, and punctuation corrections. Hand it in for the final evaluation and grade.

Defending a Position

In this unit you will learn about pro-con and academic-argument research writing. You will first write a short pro-con research paper and then expand that paper into a longer academic-argument paper.

A pro-con essay looks at ideas or issues about which people have opposing views that usually are not easily resolved. The pro side supports the issue. The con side opposes the issue. Sometimes by comparing one side with another you can decide which view you prefer.

The academic-argument research paper is one of the most common types of paper you will be asked to write in college. Academic-argument papers write briefly about both sides of the issue, and then the rest of the paper defends only one side, pro or con. You will argue by giving facts, telling observations, showing cause and/or effect, and using comparison and/or contrast. Your goal will be to convince your reader that of all the opinions that may be formed about the topic, yours is the most logical.

In this unit you will:

▼ Use all the writing and library skills you have learned

▼ Write a pro-con research paper

▼ Write an academic-argument research paper

You will also learn to:

▼ Use additional transitions and modal verbs

▼ Write APA headings and abstracts

Other skills you will practice are:

▼ Writing about two sides of an issue without showing your opinion (pro and con)

▼ Supporting your opinion with facts, examples, and statistics (academic argument

CHAPTER 17

Pro-Con: Looking at Both Sides

Pro means favoring or **supporting** an idea or an issue.

Con means being against or **opposing** an idea or an issue.

A pro-con essay or research paper gives facts supporting both sides of an issue. The writer stands in the middle, making observations and stating facts that support both sides equally. The writer does not state an opinion.

This is the position of the writer of a pro-con paper:

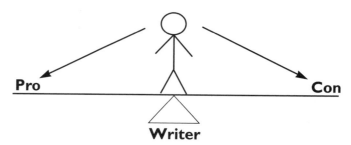

Pro   Con

Writer

Examples of pro-con issues:

Abortion

Pro: Yes, a woman has the right to abort an unwanted pregnancy.

Con: No, an unborn child has the right to live.

Nuclear power

Pro: Yes, nuclear power is the energy that will preserve our natural resources.

Con: No, nuclear power is more dangerous than helpful.

Gun control

Pro: Yes, guns need to be controlled because too many people misuse them.

Con: No, American citizens have the right to own guns as guaranteed by the Bill of Rights.

PART 1 *Organizing Pro-Con Papers*

There are several ways to organize the paragraphs in the main part of a pro-con paper. Two ways are shown below. Of course, the introduction and conclusion are similar to those in other papers you have written.

Read the following essay entitled "Deer Hunt: Good or Bad" and follow the directions.

▼ Circle the hook.

▼ Underline the thesis statement in the introduction.

▼ Underline the topic sentences in each paragraph.

▼ Put a minus (-) in the margin next to the *con* statements.

▼ Put a plus (+) in the margin next to the *pro* statements.

▼ Answer the questions below.

Example 1

Deer Hunt: Good or Bad?

The deer hunt is very popular in Utah. It is so popular that schools are closed on the Friday the official deer hunt begins. Although there are many people who actually go into the mountains to hunt, many do not. As well as having a fun vacation, people who hunt use it as an excuse to drink liquor, have parties, and shoot at anything that moves. As a result, each year hunters die from gun wounds. Some people wonder if this hunt is really necessary.

Some wildlife experts say that it is very necessary. During the winter, natural food for the deer is scarce. If their numbers were allowed to grow without "the hunt," many of the animals would die of starvation. So the hunt is necessary to control the numbers that must survive the harsh winters.

From another point of view, however, the deer were here before people. Not surviving the winter was nature's way of eliminating the sick and weak from the herd. Those deer that survived were the strongest, so their babies would also be strong. Therefore, there was a natural building of a strong species of deer.

It could be that the hunt is killing off the strong ones who are needed to strengthen the deer population as a whole. Perhaps the hunt is more to satisfy people's need for adventure than to save the deer. Perhaps it is part of both reasons.

1. Which paragraph is *for* the deer hunt?_____

2. Which paragraph is *against* the deer hunt?_____

3. List the transitions that the writer uses.

   _____

   _____

Example 2

Read the following essay entitled "Soccer at Our College" and follow the directions.

▼ Circle the hook.

▼ Underline the thesis statement in the introduction.

▼ Underline the topic sentences in each paragraph.

▼ Put a minus (-) in the margin next to the *con* statements.

▼ Put a plus (+) in the margin next to the *pro* statements.

▼ Answer the questions below.

Soccer at Our College

The most popular game, soccer, is played on every continent in the world. This game can be played almost anywhere, with little equipment. All you need are some willing contestants, a ball, and a place to play. Even though soccer is a universal sport, the athletic department of our college does not want to sponsor an official soccer team.

The biggest reason our college does not want to sponsor soccer is financial. The money in the budget is not sufficient for two teams, and to be fair there must be a team of men and a team of women. Furthermore, it costs a lot of money for teams to travel to play other colleges. The administration fears that soccer teams might spend a lot of money that is now used for other important sports programs. On the other hand, this year the men's team is making enough money to finance their own program by selling game tickets. Since several local colleges want to expand their schedules to include our college, and since our college would have two teams, there would be more games. Having more games with nearby colleges means larger crowds and more ticket sales. The soccer teams may almost be able to finance themselves.

Another big problem is providing equal opportunity for men and women in sports. So, while there is a men's team, the athletic department says women are not interested in playing college soccer. But the students think there are a lot of women who want to play soccer because the present intramural competition includes some women's teams. There are probably enough serious players on these teams to make an official college team.

In addition, playing space for additional games is difficult to find. Most observers would agree that there is no place on our college campus to have two soccer fields. However, the schedule could be arranged so that the women and men could share the present playing field. For official games they could alternate using the field on Friday and Saturday afternoons and evenings. This would use the field efficiently and no new space would be needed.

In short, the athletic department has good reasons to refuse to sponsor soccer. But there are also good reasons to support a soccer program. Only time will tell whether soccer gains enough support to be played as an official college sport at our college.

1. Fill in the following chart with the pro and con points in the soccer essay.

Pro: Yes, soccer should be official.	**Con:** No, soccer should not be official.

2. Did this article influence you to form an opinion about the problem? What is your opinion?

_____

_____

3. List the transitions that are used in this article.

_____

_____

PART 2 *Pro-Con Models*

Pro-con papers use facts, logic, and opinions of experts to show both sides of an issue. Here are two possible ways to organize the main paragraphs of this kind of paper.

Model 1 was used in the "Deer Hunt: Good or Bad?" essay. After the introduction, the next paragraph talked about one side of the issue and the following paragraph talked about the other side of the issue.

Model 2 was used in the "Soccer in Our College" essay. In this form, each paragraph between the introduction and conclusion talked about both sides of the issue. In other words, a single paragraph showed both sides of one part of the topic. This form is good for longer papers.

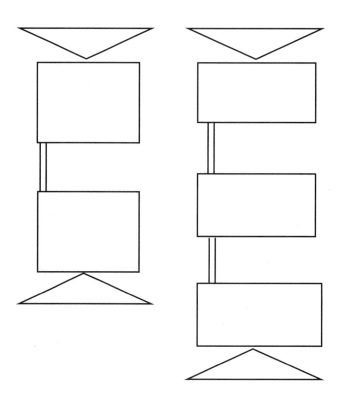

Models 1 and 2 look like this:

Model 1	**Model 2**
I. Introduction	I. Introduction
II. Pro	II. (Major division)
A.	A. Pro
B.	B. Con
C.	
	Transition
Transition	
	III. (Major division)
III. Con	A. Pro
A.	B. Con
B.	
C.	Transition
IV. Conclusion	IV. (Major division)
	A. Pro
	B. Con
	V. Conclusion

PRACTICE 1

Using Pro-Con Models

Follow these steps:

▼ Choose one pro-con subject from the list below.

   1. People should marry after age 30.

   2. Television should be banned from homes.

   3. College students should have cars.

   4. Parents should spank their children.

   5. Steady dating should begin after age 18.

▼ Write the pro-con topic on the line and complete the chart to show the arguments on both sides. Try to find the opposite sides for each point.

Pro-con topic _____

Watch Your Language

English Should Be Official
By Bradley S. O'Leary

No other country has been able to assimilate so many people, from so many backgrounds, for so long a time as the USA.

What draws immigrants to America's shores today is the same as it was in the days of Ellis Island: religious, political, and economic freedom—all of which are possible because there are more ties that bind us than misunderstandings that divide us. The strongest of those ties is a common language. That language is English.

Many Americans are surprised to learn that English is not our official language. English is the official language of 14 other countries, yet not ours. English also is the language that 90 percent of immigrants' children speak. It is the language of 80 percent of the world's electronic databases and communications networks. Yet some politicians oppose making our common language our official language. English has been our common language for more than 200 years, but its future as our common language is threatened by those who court ethnic groups by spending tax dollars to Balkanize our language.

Making English official wouldn't mean: "If you can't speak the language, get out." It would mean the government encourages the learning of English and stresses that it's vital to speak English to reap the benefits of American life and contribute to America.

A common language fosters growth and understanding. We can be taught by others only if we can understand what they say.

With out-of-control government costs in the news, we must address the exorbitant price of multilingualism. Last year, politicians in L.A. spent $900,000 to translate voting documents into seven languages.

Just look north for an example of how expensive multilingualism is. Canada, with one-tenth our population, spends $6 billion a year translating into two languages. The USA, with nearly 150 ethnic languages, could see the costs of multilingualism reach many billions of dollars more. The costs of civil fragmentation defy economic calculations.

The USA has become the planet's oldest democracy because of its ability to absorb, rather than accommodate, immigrants. We should accept legal immigrants only if they accept the responsibility of learning our laws, our language, and our way of life.

English Shouldn't Be Official
By Victor Kamber

If "English-Only" proponents would put half their resources into increasing opportunities for immigrants to learn English, rather than into oppressive, pointless legislation, they would solve whatever problems non-English speakers may cause society.

But that isn't the point. They aren't interested in solving problems. They are cynically using "English only" to whip up anti-immigrant frenzy for political gain, exploiting our ugliest instincts.

We don't need a law formalizing what already is a fact: English is the language in which this nation's business is conducted. English somehow has maintained this status through endless immigration. In spite of the hysteria of the "English-only" Chicken Littles, the sky hasn't fallen and the republic hasn't collapsed.

Any immigrant smart enough to get into this country is smart enough to realize that a good command of English is essential to success. Immigrants work hard to learn the language. But we lack the resources to accommodate the high demand. In New York City this year, 35,000 to 40,000 students were enrolled in adult English classes but 50,000 had to be put on the waiting list. This is the real scandal.

Making English our official language won't help. And it would do real damage. For example: The testimony of crime victims who can't yet speak English might be prohibited in court. Police officers and doctors might be left without the interpreters they rely on to protect people who don't speak English. Schools might find it more difficult to communicate with pupils' parents.

A failure to pass "English-only" laws would benefit all, because multilingualism will help the USA compete in the new global economy. While we must give every immigrant access to English classes, let's not inhibit the use of other languages. In most of the rest of the world, educated people speak more than one language. The more Spanish speakers in the USA, the better we can compete in Latin America. The more speakers of Asian languages, the better we can compete in the Pacific Rim.

Immigrants are a resource for economic development, not a burden. They should be cultivated, not bashed.

(Used by permission of Bradley S. O'Leary and Victor Kamber.)

PART 4 *Unit Five Assignment 1—Pro-Con Research Paper*

In this assignment you will:

▼ use all the research skills you have learned in the last three papers

▼ share research and organizing information with another classmate

▼ have more freedom in choosing your topic and your sources

I. GETTING STARTED (Do with your partner.)   Due: _____

    A. Choose a partner.

    B. Decide on a pro-con issue that you are both interested in. This is important since you will be working on the same topic for your pro-con and academic-argument papers.

    C. Choose a topic of your own with teacher approval or choose one of the topics below.

    D. Subject headings are included in parentheses. They will help you start your research at the library.

        People should be vegetarians. (Diet, Nutrition, Health)
        Advertising should be controlled. (Marketing, Psychology)
        Men and women are equal. (Rights, Psychology)
        Marijuana should be legal in the United States. (Drugs, Health, Law, Medicine, Rights)
        Movies and TV programs cause violence in society. (Sociology, Psychology, Communication)
        The United States should have an open immigration policy. (Law, Economics, Sociology)
        A thin person is a healthy person. (Diet, Health, Nutrition)
        Nuclear power plants should be banned. (Energy, Environment)

    E. Create a pro-con statement that has two defensible sides.

II. PREWRITING (Do with your partner.)   Due: _____

    A. Discuss all your ideas about the topic with your partner.

    B. Use "Pro and Con Prewriting Worksheet" to brainstorm some major points to perhaps use as headings on both sides of your topic.

    C. Add any subpoints you both can think of.

III. GATHERING INFORMATION (Do with your partner.) Due: _____

    A. Decide with your partner where you might find the best information about the main points.

    B. Divide the work equally and set a time or date to have the work done.

C. Do the research to find facts, examples, and evidence to support your major points on both sides of the topic.

D. Write the facts, examples, and evidence on note cards.

1. Write key words on the cards that match the main points on your worksheet.

2. Write your initials on your own note cards.

E. If you find a lot of valuable information in an area you didn't think about before, add major points to your individual worksheet and discuss this new information with your partner.

IV. ORGANIZING THE INFORMATION   Due: _____
(Do alone and with your partner.)

A. Discuss the information both of you have found. (You may want to photocopy your partner's note cards.)

B. Together, choose the best major points and decide on a key word or phrase for each major point.

C. Look at all the note cards and divide them into two groups: information that might be useful to support your major points and information that might not be useful. Put the cards that are probably not going to be useful aside. Do not throw them away as you may want some of them later.

D. Make sure each note card has a key word.

(*Note*: Some information might be useful for both the pro side and the con side.)

E. Put all the cards with the same key words together.

F. Divide the note cards into a group for the pro outline and a group for the con outline.

G. Use the cards to help you write one outline that combines both sides in one paper.

H. Make sure each of you has a copy of the completed outline.

V. WRITING OR TYPING THE FIRST DRAFT (Do alone.) Due: _____

A. Each of you will use the same outline to write your own first draft of a complete pro-con paper.

B. Each of you will also have your own title page, typed outline, and reference page.

VI. REVISING AND REWRITING   Due: _____
(Do alone and with your partner.)

A. Exchange papers with your partner. Check for form and accuracy of information.

B. Exchange papers with another classmate and evaluate each other's papers. Use the "Peer Evaluation for Unit Five Pro-Con Research Paper" on pages 168–169.

C. Reorganize the outline and paper as necessary and retype it.

D. Hand in all note cards, photocopies, title page, paper, and reference list. Your teacher will edit your work.

VII. EDITING AND REWRITING (Do alone.)   Due: _____

Make the final corrections on the paper and retype.
(Don't throw away your note cards! You will need them for the next assignment.)

Preparing the folder to turn in:

Put your completed research paper in a three-hole pocket folder. Make sure that the pages are in this order:

1. Title page

2. Final outline

3. Research paper

4. Reference list

Place these items in the pockets of the folder:

1. Planning outline

2. Photocopies

3. Note cards

4. First draft

PRACTICE 3

Pro-Con Prewriting Worksheet

▼ Write your pro-con statement on a piece of paper.

▼ With your partner, brainstorm the pros and cons of your issue.

▼ Write them in columns with pros at the left and cons at the right.

▼ Circle the items you think will become your main headings.

Transitions that show the cause of something can also be used to give the reasons for something. You have already used transitions for cause-and-effect and comparison-and-contrast research papers. These transitions are also useful in process research papers.

PART 5 *Pro-Con Transitions*

Uses of Transitions

To explain or give a reason

for   because   since   as   because of   due to   so that   in order to

Example:

> **Since** freedom of speech is a part of the Constitution of the United States every immigrant should be allowed to speak his or her native language whenever and wherever he or she chooses. **Due to** the fact that it is hard to find work if you can't understand English, people will discover on their own that **in order to** be paid well, they will have to learn English. For the U.S. government to make everyone learn English violates our freedom of speech.

To explain a result

as a result of	as a consequence	therefore	thus
the reason for	consequently	because	so
for these reasons	because of these reasons		

Examples:

> **As a result of** the U.S. government possibly making English official, government papers will not be printed in any other language. **Therefore,** this will save the tax-payers money.

To show an exception or an alternative

although	instead of	except	if	in spite of
even though	yet	otherwise	unless	still
while				

Examples:

> **Instead of** requiring all people who live in the U.S. to know English, perhaps it should only be required if the person wishes to become a citizen. **If** this were the case, maybe the argument would stop.
>
> **In spite of** some efforts to stop the English-only movement, lawmakers are becoming more and more in favor of the idea. **Unless** freedom-loving groups unite to educate the public, the freedom to use one's native language in every situation will be lost.
>
> Freedom-loving groups must work together. **Otherwise,** English will become the official language sooner than they think.
>
> **While** it is important to save money, it is more important to save our freedom of speech.

To introduce a generalization

as a general rule   in general   generally

Examples:

> **As a general rule,** the majority of people who live in the U.S. speak English at home, at work, at school, and play.

To establish reasonable certainty

obviously   naturally   certainly   unquestionably

admittedly   of course   even now   surely

Examples:

> **Unquestionably,** a person from another country who lives and works in the U.S. will want to learn the English language. **Even now,** many immigrants try to learn English as quickly as possible.

PRACTICE 4

Adding Transitions

▼ Read the following paragraphs from pro-con essays written by students.

▼ Write an appropriate transition in each blank. The words in parentheses tell which category of transition you need.

Paragraph 1

> **From a pro-con paper about illegal immigration:**
>
> *(Additional information)* _____ the problem faced by the people of the U.S. is the loss of a good environment. *(Examples)* _____ Los Angeles suffers the worst air pollution in the country. The governor of California said that it could cost $12,000,000,000 per year by the year 2000 in order to improve the environment (Grant, 1991). *(Additional information)* _____ the population in L.A. is still growing because of the number of immigrants who continue to come into that city.
>
> *(Mario Diaz—Guatemala)*

Paragraph 2

> **From a pro-con paper about the rights of animals:**
>
> *(Exception)* _____ the contributions of animals are substantial for human life, opponents believe that animals should be protected by laws and the killing of animals should be forbidden. *(Result)* _____ concerned people have organized pro-animal-rights groups, *(example)* _____ People for Ethical Treatment of Animals (PETA), GreenPeace, and the Animal Liberation Front.
>
> *(Mayumi Goto—Japan)*

PART 6   *Evaluations for Your Pro-Con Research Paper*

Evaluation 1

Self-Evaluation

Because this pro-con paper was done with a classmate, it is important that you evaluate the amount of work you did for the success of the paper. Use the following questions to evaluate your own contirbution to the paper.

Name of student _____ Points possible: 50

1. How much time (hours) did I spend in the library doing the research? _____

2. How many note cards did I make? _____

3. How much time did I spend helping to organize the information? _____

- Combining note cards _____

- Dividing them into pro and con groups _____

- Writing the planning outline _____

Evaluation 2

Peer Evaluation of Pro-Con Research Paper

You often learn more about the strengths and weaknesses of your own writing by evaluating the writing of a classmate. Therefore, exchange papers and this evaluation form with a classmate. Read his or her paper carefully and mark the following points. Put **S** for Satisfactory and **U** for Unsatisfactory in the blank. Write the total number of **S**s and **U**s at the top.

Name of writer _____   Total *S*'s _____
Name of evaluator_____   Total *U*'s_____
Date_____

_____   1. Title page exists and the form is correct.
_____   2. Outline page exists and is typed in the correct form, single-spaced.
_____   3. Paper is typed (two–four pages).
_____   4. Introduction has three parts: hook, general information, thesis statement.
_____   5. Hook is unusual or very interesting.
_____   6. Thesis statement clearly states the issue and both sides of that issue.
_____   7. The main idea for each paragraph is clear and stated in the topic sentence.
_____   8. Each point has good supporting details, facts, and examples.
_____   9. Transitions join one paragraph to another.
_____ 10. Transitions show relationship of supporting details to the main ideas.
_____ 11. Transitions are used with the correct meanings.

_____ 12. Both sides of the issue are treated fairly.
_____ 13. Conclusion shows thesis statment ideas.
_____ 14. Conclusion has three parts: thesis statement, summary of main points, and final statement.
_____ 15. Citations exist and follow APA style.
_____ 16. Most of the citations are summary or paraphrase (only one or two quotations).
_____ 17. Reference page exists with the correct title.
_____ 18. References follow the APA style.
_____ 19. Note cards exist and follow the form of the model on page 132.

Tell the writer what you liked about the paper.

_____

_____

What ideas would improve this paper?

_____

_____

Write your second draft by making the revisions that were suggested. Hand it in for editing corrections.

Write your third draft by making the grammar, spelling, and punctuation corrections. Hand it in for the final evaluation and grade.

Defending Your Position

INTRODUCTION

In this chapter you will expand your pro-con paper to an academic-argument paper on the same topic. You will be able to use a lot of the research you have already done on your pro-con paper, but you will not use your pro-con outline. You must reorganize the material and make a new outline to show academic argument. This academic-argument paper assignment, which is your final library research paper for this course, will also include an abstract and APA headings.

PART 1 *The Academic Argument*

An academic-argument or position paper is one that states a clear opinion of one side of an issue and supports that opinion with logical reasoning, facts, explanations, and reliable opinions of others. The audience is more interested in how convincingly you support your opinion than in the actual side you take.

The first step in writing any paper is to pick a topic. When choosing a topic for an academic-argument paper, you must be sure that:

- it has two strong opposing sides, one of which you agree with

- the defense of your position is interesting and varied, but not too complicated for a short five-page paper

Academic-argument papers use many of the organizational models you have learned in this course (summary report, cause-and-effect, comparison-and-contrast, and pro-con). In showing your side of the issue, you must use the models that will best explain your point of view. No matter what model you use, you must make a clear connection between your opinion and the facts and avoid using emotional reasoning.

Therefore, as you research and write your academic-argument paper, you must make sure that you have:

- given enough facts, reasons, and details to make your view believable

- included facts or reasons that are logical and clearly related to defending one side of the topic

- explained the details of the facts or reasons (not just listed them)

- answered the research question without getting off the actual topic

Academic-argument papers should use formal language and avoid over-generalizing words, such as *always* and *never.* Unsupported feelings do not belong in this type of paper because facts and ideas, not emotions, prove your opinion.

Transitions become very important in an academic-argument paper. They help the reader follow your reasoning and your proof. If transitions are lacking, the reader will have a hard time seeing relationships of one idea to another in your argument. Also, transitions are an important part of the formal language necessary in an academic-argument paper.

When writing this type of paper, assume that no one knows enough about the subject to agree with your position. You must not only educate but convince the reader that your position is correct. By taking this attitude, your paper will be more effective.

Finally, a strong conclusion in an academic-argument paper is vital. If the reasoning in the body of the paper is presented in a clear, convincing order, the summary of the main points and your resulting opinion will also be strong. If the body of the paper is weak, the conclusion will be weak as well, and the reader will not be convinced or even sympathetic to your position.

PRACTICE 1

Listing What You Learned

▼ Write down ten facts that you have learned about academic-argument papers.

1. *The topic I pick must be an issue that has two strong opinions or sides.*

2. _____

3. _____

4. _____

5. _____

6. _____

7. _____

8. _____

9. _____

10. _____

PRACTICE 2

Looking at an

Argument

▼ Read the following argument essay. How does the writer try to convince you to eat dirt?

Eat Dirt!

As our lives become busier, good nutrition and money are often sacrificed. It is all too easy to stop by a vending machine or fast-food restaurant for a quick, but expensive meal. Dirt is a reasonable solution to the problem and it can be a very important part of your diet.

First, soil is easy to find and it is very inexpensive. Bucketful after bucketful can be found in your own garden or practically anywhere. In addition to being readily available, most soil is free.

Second, not only is dirt free, but it is also full of nutrients. The human body requires certain minerals that are essential for health. Among these important minerals are iron, copper, and zinc (Zimmerman, 1992). Lambert and Linch (1991) cite studies carried out by the National Soil Society in which 20-milligram soil samples taken from every state in the union showed enough traces of iron, copper, and zinc to meet or exceed the U.S.R.D.A. daily requirements.

Third, and perhaps the most important of all, many people find that soil has a pleasant taste. In a recent survey conducted by the Department of Food and Nutrition at Cook Well University, 49 out of 50 students rated traditional recipes substituting dirt for flour as tasting superior to the recipes made in the traditional way with flour. In fact, many students admitted they enjoyed eating dirt all by itself (Johnson, 1992).

In sum, dirt can be a viable option for our busy, yet poor lifestyles. It is probably faster to fill a cup full of dirt from the front yard than to go to the local McDonald's. It is certainly less expensive and probably more nutritious.

(Used by permission of Sarah Johnson)

References

Johnson, S. (1993, March 2). Dirt rated number one. <u>The Daily Blab</u>, pp. 4,8.

Lambert, L., & Linch, R. (1991). Mineral levels in soil samples. <u>American Journal of Soil</u>, 2, 22-25.

Zimmermann, K. (1992). <u>The healthy diet</u>. New York: Macnothing.

PART 2 *Academic-Argument Models*

So far you have learned about the organizational patterns for comparison and contrast, cause and effect, and pro-con. Academic-argument papers also have organizational patterns that can be illustrated with models. Some models for academic arguments are below:

Model 1

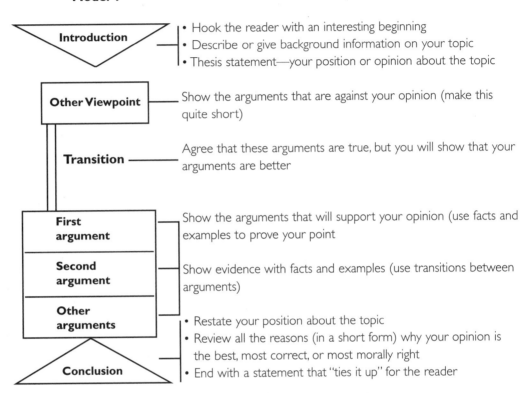

Introduction
- Hook the reader with an interesting beginning
- Describe or give background information on your topic
- Thesis statement—your position or opinion about the topic

Other Viewpoint — Show the arguments that are against your opinion (make this quite short)

Transition — Agree that these arguments are true, but you will show that your arguments are better

First argument — Show the arguments that will support your opinion (use facts and examples to prove your point

Second argument — Show evidence with facts and examples (use transitions between arguments)

Other arguments

Conclusion
- Restate your position about the topic
- Review all the reasons (in a short form) why your opinion is the best, most correct, or most morally right
- End with a statement that "ties it up" for the reader

Model 2

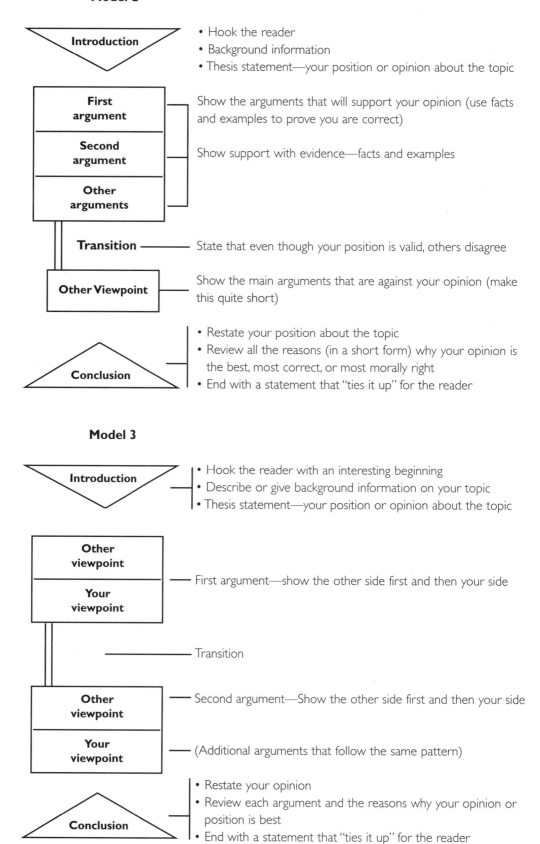

Introduction
- Hook the reader
- Background information
- Thesis statement—your position or opinion about the topic

First argument

Second argument

Other arguments

Show the arguments that will support your opinion (use facts and examples to prove you are correct)

Show support with evidence—facts and examples

Transition ——— State that even though your position is valid, others disagree

Other Viewpoint ——— Show the main arguments that are against your opinion (make this quite short)

Conclusion
- Restate your position about the topic
- Review all the reasons (in a short form) why your opinion is the best, most correct, or most morally right
- End with a statement that "ties it up" for the reader

Model 3

Introduction
- Hook the reader with an interesting beginning
- Describe or give background information on your topic
- Thesis statement—your position or opinion about the topic

Other viewpoint

Your viewpoint

——— First argument—show the other side first and then your side

——— Transition

Other viewpoint

Your viewpoint

——— Second argument—Show the other side first and then your side

——— (Additional arguments that follow the same pattern)

Conclusion
- Restate your opinion
- Review each argument and the reasons why your opinion or position is best
- End with a statement that "ties it up" for the reader

PRACTICE 3

Sample Academic-Argument Essay

▼ Read the following essay and decide what model it uses.

▼ Underline all the transitions.

Early Steady Dating

Young people in the U.S. are steady-dating too early. Some even constantly date the same person from as young as 13 years old. Some people think that this trend is fine because everyone has the right to choose when to begin dating and for how long. But more and more professionals who work with teenagers are saying that early dating damages social development, causes false love, and creates early, unstable marriages.

Developing socially is a very important part of becoming a contributing member of society. Having many friends of both sexes has been seen as a vital factor in this social development. People who group-date during their teens or who date many different people before they finally get married seem to have a variety of friends during their adult life, can relate to other people in more positive and accepting ways, and have a more lasting relationship in their marriage. If a young teenager focuses socially on only one person, a type of social handicap can occur because only one person is the major stimulus for learning how to get along with others.

Usually the cause of early steady-dating is that one or both of the partners have unmet love needs; therefore, they develop a dependency that is misinterpreted as true love. Perhaps their parents were divorced or abusive, so they did not feel the love that is necessary for a healthy self-image. They find someone who fills those strong needs and they become emotionally bonded to that person to the exclusion of all others. This is a very dangerous situation because the teen years are a time of numerous emotional and physical changes. These changes may not occur in both people at the same time, or the changes in emotional needs may conflict so that one person in the couple suddenly becomes disinterested in the other. Therefore, a person who bonds with a partner early could very well be abruptly abandoned for someone else. This abandonment might cause further damage to the person's self-value, and he or she will go looking for someone else who can fill the growing and driving need for love.

There is also a danger of marrying too young and having children too soon in these early steady-dating situations. Because the emotional bond that young people feel may be misinterpreted as love, teen marriage sometimes occurs—often against the better judgment of parents and older friends and even some peers. The young people might argue, "Aren't we able to choose for ourselves? Have you forgotten what true love really is?" The arguments continue until they get their way or run away to get married.

In a marriage based on false love, the emotional entanglements become even more complex. What was thought to be a solution now becomes a complex problem. She is left at home alone with the baby while he goes off to a job he must have because they have bills to pay. He might go out with the boys in the evening, something he never did before because he was going out with only her.

Moreover, he was the only one she cared to know and associate with during high school, but now she begins thinking about the boys in her class who are preparing for a profession or vocation and wondering "How would it have been if . . . ?" Therefore, because of the false expectations before marriage and the reality of the situation after marriage, both people could feel betrayed and even more lonely and unloved. In young marriages, "growing up together" is so painful that divorce is very likely.

Although there is strong evidence against early steady-dating, those who are against any age restraints claim that they are defending a young person's right to choose. They say that establishing an age for steady-dating is damaging to the ego of young people and causes rebellion. Rather than more rules, they say that youth need more freedom so that better adult-youth relationships can develop. In other words, when adults respond to the pressure of teens to do what they want, peace will reign. These claims may have some degree of truth, but total freedom is not the answer to the problems caused by steady-dating too young.

In conclusion, early steady-dating can be detrimental to a young person's social development. Furthermore, relationships based on false love often result in early marriage, which throws young people into the raw realities of the demands of family. The marriage becomes unstable, and divorce occurs. Research and experience teach that having an age limit for steady-dating is not only wise, but highly advisable.

PART 3 *Unit Five Assignment 2: Academic-Argument Research Paper*

As you work through this assignment, you will learn to:

▼ Use major division and subdivision headings within your paper

▼ Write an abstract for your paper in place of the outline

▼ Use modals as you prove that your position is correct

Your assignment for this paper will be different from previous papers. This is because you did some of the important steps for an academic-argument paper when you wrote the pro-con paper. You have already finished steps I and II, Getting Started and Prewriting. Now you are ready for the steps that follow.

I. GETTING STARTED

II. PREWRITING

III. GATHERING INFORMATION

Decide which side of your pro-con paper you wish to defend. Look over all the note cards you and your partner have and select those that best support your side. You will also need a few facts to show the opposing point of view. In addition, you might need to do some more research on your side. For the rest of this assignment, you will work alone, not with a partner.

IV. ORGANIZING THE INFORMATION   Due: _____

Use the cards along with your own knowledge and experience to write an outline that follows one of the academic-argument patterns.

V. WRITING YOUR FIRST DRAFT   Due: _____

A. Write a formal introduction with your strong opinion in the thesis statement.
B. Use citations for all the facts you use from the note cards.
C. Use enough facts or examples to support each reason in your argument.
D. Use transitions to show your reasoning process.

VI. REVISING AND RETYPING   Due: _____

A. After a peer evaluation of your first draft, make any necessary revisions.
  1. Add details, examples, and explanations to make your argument clearer.
  2. Reorganize to make your argument stronger.
  3. Improve paragraphing.
B. Add APA headings and subheadings.
C. Write a short abstract for your paper.

VII. EDITING AND RETYPING   Due: _____

A. Correct errors in grammar, spelling, and punctuation.
B. Use the spell-check feature on your word processor.

Preparing the folder to turn in:

A. Put the paper in a three-hole pocket folder. Make sure the pages are in this order:
  1. Title page
  2. Abstract page
  3. Paper
  4. Reference list
B. Place these items in the pockets of the folder:
  1. Photocopies of the articles you used
  2. Cards with a rubber band around them—all the bibliography and note cards you actually used. Put them in the order used in the paper.
  3. First draft
  4. Other drafts of the paper

P A R T 4 *Stating Opinions with Modals*

Because most academic-argument papers discuss issues on which people have opinions one way or the other, modals play a very important part in trying to convince the reader about a certain position. Modals that are commonly used to persuade or argue are:

can	may	should	will	must
could	might	ought to	would	have to

The following chart and examples show the meaning and use of modals for academic-argument writing.

For an opinion or possibility   **may, might, can, could**

Different government laws **may (might, can, could)** have an effect on the number of legal immigrants.

For degrees of possibility, if the conditions are met

Weak possibility   **may, might, can, could**

A new law **might** create future problems.

Moderate possibility   **would**

The citizens **would** be quite upset if there were a great change in immigration policies.

Strong possibility   **will**

Illegal immigration **will** spread if authorities are not given greater power.

For a strong opinion   **should, ought to**

Immigration **should (ought to)** be controlled in order to make sure that there are jobs for Americans who pay taxes.

For a strong need   **must** (Formal) **have to**
(Informal)

In order to make sure that there are jobs for Americans, immigration **must** be controlled. People **have to** become educated about the types of jobs available.

Negative forms of modals also have a very strong influence on an argument and can be used in academic-argument writing as well. Here are some that might help strengthen your paper.

Not advisable or possible   may not, might not, shouldn't

The new legislature **may not (might not)** want to pay for more police officers to control gangs, but they **shouldn't** change the programs they have already approved.

Strongly not advisable or possible   wouldn't

It **wouldn't** be a good idea for citizens to take up arms against these gangs.

Impossible   can't, won't

We **can't** have gangs controlling our cities!

New laws **won't** have any effect unless there is some way to enforce them.

PRACTICE 4

Recognizing Modals in Arguments

The following paragraphs are from a paper about euthanasia. Euthanasia is helping someone to die who is terminally ill.

▼ Read each paragraph.

▼ Circle all the modals.

▼ Write the meaning of the modal in the margin. Refer to Part 4.

Euthanasia

Paragraph 1

Supporters of euthanasia emphasize that euthanasia should be legalized. But a patient's trust in the doctor's wholehearted service would be hard to maintain if doctors are licensed to kill patients (Leon, 1988). Suppose that you are old, homeless, in poor health, and alone in the world. Maybe you are brought to a free hospital. Since doctors have the right to kill you, you may not be able to sleep at night, being fearful that a nurse or intern may enter with a syringe full of lethal medicine. Even if a nurse comes in with a syringe full of penicillin, it would be difficult for you to believe him or her. Lack of trust may make other treatments less effective, too. As a consequence, fewer patients would receive the care they really need. So legalization of euthanasia should not be accepted.

Paragraph 2

If euthanasia is legalized, it would bring destruction to the autonomy and dignity of humankind. For example, doctors might be given supreme power over their patients' lives, especially when the patients are unable to think for themselves, such as those in a comatose state or with severe mental illness. That could mean that the right to choose one's own death could be changed to the right of someone else to request another's death. Doctors might also be tempted to kill their patients who suffer from terrible pain. Only the law prevents this from happening. In

Holland, where euthanasia is legal, a recent survey of 300 physicians shows that over 40 percent had performed euthanasia more than five times (Leon, 1988). If euthanasia is legalized in the United States, physicians would have the overwhelming burden of deciding when to take away the autonomy and dignity of their patients.

Paragraph 3

Lastly, if euthanasia for terminally ill people becomes legalized, the number of teenage suicides might increase. For instance, when adolescents see that it is permissible for sick people to choose to kill themselves, they may judge it to be permissible for them to do the same thing when they are in pain, even though much teenage pain is psychological rather than physical. Therefore, it will put young people in serious danger if the government accepts the legalization of euthanasia.

(Sukjin Jo—Korea)

Read your academic-argument paper carefully. Find sentences where you can improve your argument by using modals.

P A R T 5 *From Final Outline to APA Headings*

In many papers that use APA style you will not have a separate outline after the title page. Instead, the major divisions of your outline are changed to *headings* within the paper itself. As you write each part of your paper:

- put the words of your *major headings* (I, II, III, VI) in the center of the page like a title, and leave out the Roman numerals

- put the words of your *subheadings* (A, B, C, D) at the left margin, underline them, and leave out the letters

Example:

Subheadings   **Major Headings**

. . . However, there has been little if any success with this proposal. It looks as though these masculine generic terms will continue, at least during the near future. The danger in that, of course, is that readers may continue to ignore or trivialize the role of women whenever they see the generic use of *man* or *he.*

Sexism in Labels

Miss/Mrs.

Although much of the research has been focused on writing and its involvement in oppression of women, there are also many examples of the stereotyping of women in our everyday speech. One of the more obvious is the prefix change of the name of females at marriage. Whether an adult male is married or not, he is referred to as "Mister." However, a female must change from "Miss" before marriage to "Mrs." after. This . . .

Source: Hansen, K. (1989). *English 315 supplement: Second edition.* Edina, MN: Burgess International Group Inc. Bellwether Press.

Note: The introduction of your paper *does not need* an APA heading. Since it is the first part of your paper, the reader will know it is your introduction.

PRACTICE 5

Writing APA Headings

▼ Look at the paper "The Effects of Television Violence on Children" (pp. 18–25).

▼ The major headings of the outline for that paper are on the next page. Write them in the appropriate places in the paper. (Since you will be handwriting the headings, you will not be able to leave the spacing required for a typed paper.)

Outline

   I. Introduction

   II. Promotes Violent Imitative Play

  III. Teaches Obscene Language

  IV. Demonstrates That Violence Is Power

   V. Teaches Violence Solves Problems

  VI. Encourages Aggressive Behavior

 VII. Distorts Reality

VIII. Portrays a Frightening World

  IX. Conclusion

The first part of the paper is done for you below. The example begins with the introduction of the paper. Remember that the introduction does not need an APA heading.

The Effects of Television

4

The Effects of Television Violence on Children

"Television is not reflecting the world, but the world is reflecting television" (Brady, 1992, p. 50). Television is the most widespread medium that brings violence to our youngsters, and, as a matter of fact, it is not hard to imagine how many ways TV violence affects children. But it is difficult to determine the level of responsibility television has for their aggressive behavior. Some researchers say that the relationship is direct, while others maintain that children copy it from their home environment. However, most parents who are really concerned about the increase of violence in their children are the ones who do not have violent behavior in their homes. They ask themselves, "Where is the child learning this, if we are not giving him or her the example?" From recent studies we know that violent television programs do affect children's behavior.

Promotes Violent Imitative Play

Television causes children to change their creative spirit for an imitative desire that may include violent behavior. They learn to dress, act, and even think like their TV idols. For example, as a child, I used to act, talk, and even run as the "Bionic Man." I

Add APA outline headings to the first draft of your academic-argument paper.

PART 6 *Adding an Abstract*

To review, an abstract is a very short summary of the most important parts of a paper. It is written on a separate page after the title page. An abstract is about 100 words or less depending on the length of the paper and shows the:

- topic and ideas of the thesis statement

- most important parts of the paper that support the thesis statement

- conclusions of the author (or results of the study)

Your abstract should have only a few sentences. For an academic-argument, it should give your opinion and several of the arguments that support that opinion along with your conclusion. Here is the abstract for the academic-argument paper, "The Effects of Television Violence on Children":

Example:

The Effects of Television

2

Abstract

From recent studies we know that violent television programs do affect children's behavior. They promote imitative play including violence and obscene language, demonstrate that violence is the key to power and problem solving, and even push children to commit crime. Also, TV can distort feelings and portray a frightening world. Parents can help change the influence of the constant effect of television violence.

PRACTICE 6

Analyzing an Abstract

Study the abstract above and follow the directions.

▼ <u>Underline</u> the ideas of the thesis statement.

▼ Circle other main points.

▼ Draw a box around the author's conclusion.

▼ How many words are in this abstract? _____

▼ What is the title on the page? _____

▼ Where is the short title and page number? _____

▼ Where do you think the abstract would be found in a paper?

_____

_____

> **Write an abstract for your academic-argument paper.**

PART 7 *Evaluation of Academic-Argument Research Paper*

You often learn more about the strengths and weaknesses of your own writing by evaluating the writing of a classmate. Therefore, exchange papers and this evaluation form with a classmate. Read his or her paper carefully and mark the following items.

Peer Evaluation of Academic-Argument Paper

▼ Put an *S* (Satisfactory) or a *U* (Unsatisfactory) in the blank in front of each item.

▼ Write the total number of *S*'s and *U*'s at the top.

Name of writer _____   Total *S*'s _____
Name of evaluator_____   Total *U*'s _____
Date_____

_____   1. Title page exists and is in correct form.
_____   2. Abstract page exists and is in correct form.
_____   3. Report has three to five typed pages.
_____   4. Introduction has three parts: hook, general information, thesis statement.
_____   5. Hook is unusual or very interesting.
_____   6. Thesis statement strongly states the position of the writer.
_____   7. The main idea for each paragraph is clear and stated in the topic sentence.
_____   8. Each point has enough supporting details, facts, and examples.
_____   9. Transitions join one paragraph to another.
_____   10. Transitions show the relationship of ideas in each paragraph.
_____   11. Transitions are used with the correct meanings.
_____   12. Conclusion has three parts: thesis statement, summary of main points, final statement.
_____   13. Citations exist and follow APA style.
_____   14. Most of the citations are summary or paraphrase (only one or two quotations).
_____   15. Reference page exists with the correct title.
_____   16. References follow APA style.
_____   17. Page numbers and title appear on each page.
_____   18. APA headings exist and are in correct form.
_____   19. Note cards exist and are in correct form.

What did you like about this paper?

_____

_____

Was there enough proof to support the writer's opinion?   Y   N

Is there anything that might make this paper stronger or more convincing?

_____

_____

Write your second draft by making the necessary revisions that were suggested. Hand it in for editing corrections.

Write your third draft by making the grammar, spelling, and punctuation corrections. Hand it in for the final evaluation and grade.

Branching Out

Analysis is a factor in all the writing methods in this unit. The purpose of an analysis is to learn more about something complex by looking at its smaller, more understandable parts. The first method of writing presented in this unit, analysis and interpretation, is often required when writing for humanities, fine arts, or social science classes. It is a useful writing skill for science subjects as well.

The most complex method of writing, the evaluation, is a frequent requirement for any academic subject. It is based on research combined with the skills of summary, analysis, and interpretation. An evaluation requires comparison and contrast, and may even require that you defend the values you decide are important by using an academic argument.

Another important research method is to take notes while listening to someone talk about your topic. Notes can be taken from personal interviews, speeches, lectures, television, videos, or films.

This unit will help you learn to use this kind of information in your academic papers.

In this unit you will:

▼ Write an analysis and interpretation essay

▼ Write an evaluation essay

▼ Learn to write a citation for nonprint sources

You will also learn to:

▼ Interview experts about your topic

▼ Find up-to-date information from nonprint sources

▼ Take notes from nonprint sources and use them in a short research paper

Other skills you will practice are:

▼ Organizing interpretation and evaluation essays

▼ Writing references for nonprint sources

Analysis and Interpretation

In college you may be asked to analyze and interpret a work of art, a scientific method, the work of an expert in some field, an experiment, a piece of literature, a poem, an essay, or a professional article. How is the method of analysis and interpretation applied to so many different things? This chapter will help you understand the process as you analyze and interpret works of art and photos.

PART 1 *Using Analysis and Interpretation*

The purpose of an *analysis* is to learn more about something complex by looking at its smaller, more understandable parts. An analysis is factual and does not use emotional language. Analysis can be used to:

- understand the parts of an engine
- accomplish a task in the most efficient way
- understand and then solve a problem
- find characteristics of a work of art or literature

Most people analyze often without knowing that they are doing it. You have analyzed thousands of things in your life. For instance, you probably did some analysis when choosing the clothes you have on or when finding a doctor. In this course you have used analysis when writing a comparison-and-contrast paper and when choosing information for your pro-con and academic-argument papers.

The purpose of an *interpretation* is to identify what something means and what kind of overall message it is sending. For example, when you go to a doctor with a headache, the doctor examines you and then, based on what he finds, gives you an interpretation of the symptoms, or a possible cause of the headache. When police are investigating a crime, they look at the evidence they have collected and then they interpret what the evidence means. Therefore, an interpretation can be based on a combination of facts and personal feelings. Because each person writes from his or her own viewpoint, each interpretation can be different even if the paper is on the same topic.

As you practice analysis and interpretation, you will work with these questions:

What are the facts (or points) as I see them? (analysis)

What do they mean to me? (interpretation)

PART 2 *Individual Interpretation*

To see all the varieties of personal viewpoints is one of the most interesting parts of analysis and interpretation. Even when authors are writing about the same topic, their work will be different because each person has his or her own ideas about what the details mean.

Here are some comments using analysis and interpretation about the painting below, *Farm at Chambon Sur Lac* by Marc Chagall. As you read, notice how each interpretation is different.

(Used with permission from Museum Boymans-van Beunigen, Rotterdam)

(c) 1993 ARS, New York/ADAGP, Paris

Interpretation 1

Ah! Where did you get that Chagall?

I love Chagall because he suspends reality. When we think of the earth, we think of "terra firma"—the firm earth in which the houses are all straight and level and predictable. But life isn't necessarily that way and Chagall shows us a world that isn't what we expect. He changes the usual angles of the buildings and moves windows to unnatural places. He also has a wall with no door, a wagon with only three wheels, and a water drain that goes nowhere. This is like life. Things can happen that we don't expect, not just physically, but metaphysically. What we think of as solid and real turns into illusion.

(Joyce Kohler—Adapted and used by permission.)

Interpretation 2

Chagall and Death Symbolism

Chagall uses a lot of symbolism, and in the painting *Farm at Chambon Sur Lac* there are many things that symbolize death. The first symbol is the tombstone right up against a building or wall. But it is not clear where the graveyard is. Maybe the dead people are under the feet of the living people, because the stones of the street are about the size and shape of the top of a man's head. It looks as if they made the whole street of skulls. Perhaps the grave marker is really predicting the death of all the people living behind the wall of a Jewish ghetto, because many Jews who lived in ghettos were killed in World War II.

Other elements could be symbolic of death too. The ugly man wearing a mask like a clown could be making fun of the dead world underneath his feet or the dead world to come in war. The person in black carrying a basket looks like a witch, or a woman in the form of death. The birds in the sky could be black vultures coming to circle over the dead corpses. Maybe the tower of the church is falling down because religion has little power to stop people from dying. Also, there is a black shadow that has no source. Perhaps it is the "shadow of death" slowly growing on the whole scene. Symbols seem to be hiding everywhere in this picture, and yet on the surface people are doing daily activities as if they don't see death coming toward them.

PART 3 *Brainstorming Techniques*

You have already used brainstorming techniques such as making a list, Venn diagrams, and idea maps. Asking questions is another technique that is useful for an analysis-and-interpretation paper. Some types of questions you can ask are:

- *Wh-* questions

  who, what, when, where, why, how

• *Yes/No* questions

be (am, is, are, was, were)

do (do, does, did)

PRACTICE 1

Comparing Interpretations

Here is an analysis-and-interpretation essay written by a student. He was looking at a color picture of the painting *Farm at Chambon Sur Lac* by Marc Chagall. How is this interpretation different from the interpretations of this same painting that you read earlier?

▼ Read the essay.

▼ Underline the thesis statement.

▼ Draw an arrow from the thesis statement to the place where the main idea of each paragraph connects it to the thesis statement.

Farm at Chambon Sur Lac by Chagall

Pictures talk by themselves. Every picture expresses a feeling that each individual can perceive and interpret in a different way. Many times this feeling is like the vision and mood of the artist who painted it. In the case of the *Farm at Chambon Sur Lac,* the artist wants to expose a pure combination of sentiment and technique through this little village or farm, probably situated in France.

The author involves the viewer in the sentiment of a complete atmosphere of serenity. The sky and the clouds give the sensation of a rainy day, and this provokes an image of tranquility. Also, the action that is being developed in the picture brings about the same feeling. The people in the picture, probably performing activities that are usual in their daily lives, are a perfect example of this sentiment because no one is portraying excitement.

The techniques used in this picture support the perfect harmony of this feeling of serenity. To illustrate this idea, all the colors used, or at least the majority, are cold. The buildings, the clouds, and even one person have dark, cool colors. These colors of gray, black, blue, green enforce the calm feeling of this picture.

Without technique there is no sentiment. The combination of both creates the atmosphere of the picture that communicates the final feeling in the viewer— peace.

(Marco Castello—Chile)

PRACTICE 2

Using the Analysis-and-Interpretation Process

▼ Study this photograph.

▼ Follow Steps 1 through 8 of the analysis-and-interpretation process below to write your own interpretation essay.

▼ Remember, everyone will have a different interpretation, so don't worry about getting it right because there is no right answer. What you should decide on are the major points you see and find specific support for those points.

Steps for Analysis-and-Interpretation Process

Step 1: Getting Started

A. Look at the picture above and write down the obvious information.

What is this about? _____

Where is it?_____

When was this done? _____

Who is its creator?_____

Step 2: Prewriting

A. Get a first impression. Use any words that come to your mind.

What does this picture mean to me? _____

_____

What do I feel?_____

_____

What do I think? _____

_____

B. Preparing for a thesis statement.

What does the creator of the picture want you to see?_____

_____

What is important to you in this picture?_____

_____

What do you think the meaning of the picture could be? _____

_____

C. Write a first thesis statement. _____

_____

_____

Step 3: Selecting Information

A. Analysis

What details do you see? _____

_____

_____

What details seem more important than other details? (Put an * by the

important ones.) _____

_____

What details seem to go together in groups? (Put a large circle around them.) _____

_____

B. Interpretation

What new meanings do I see?_____

_____

Is this different from my first impression? _____

_____

Do I see other details that seem to show the meaning I am discovering?

_____

_____

Do I need to make a different thesis statement? _____

_____

C. Choose several groups that seem to support your first thesis statement or a different thesis statement. Give these groups a name (heading).

Group 1: Heading _____

Group 2: Heading _____

Group 3: Heading _____

Group 4: Heading _____

Step 4: Organizing Information

A. Write a final thesis statement.

What could be the most important overall meaning of this picture to you?

_____

_____

Has it changed from your first impression? How? _____

_____

Final thesis statement _____

_____

B. Choose the groups to support the thesis statement.

What are the best three groups to show your meaning?

1. _____

2. _____

3. _____

C. Make a short planning outline.

In what order will you use these groups?

I. _____

II. _____

III. _____

Step 5: Writing the First Draft of the Essay

Write a short essay.

Step 6: Revising and Rewriting

Ask these questions:

Does the organization follow the model?

Does each paragraph support the thesis statement?

Step 7: Editing and Rewriting

Ask these questions:

Where are the grammar problems?

Where are the spelling problems?

How correct is the punctuation and capitalization?

What can I do to fix these problems?

Step 8: Evaluating

Read a classmate's essay. Compare your essay to his or hers.
Ask these questions:

Did I have my own ideas?

Were my ideas and interpretations different from any of my classmate's ideas?

PRACTICE 3

Analyzing and Interpreting
a Photograph

▼ Choose one of the photographs.

▼ Follow Steps 1 through 8 of the analysis-and-interpretation process.

▼ Write a short analysis-and-interpretation essay.

PART 5 *Unit Six Assignment—Analysis-and-Interpretation Essay*

This assignment will give you the experience of analyzing and interpreting a work of art of your choice. Follow the process you learned in the steps above.

  I. GETTING STARTED   Due: _____

      A. Find a work of art you like in a museum, a public building, a picture you find in an art book, or a magazine.

      B. Write down information about the work of art.

          1. Title of work (if there is one)

            _____

          2. Artist's name and birth/death dates

            _____

          3. Date made (if possible)

            _____

      C. Look for any other obvious or important information. (Do not research published criticism because this essay will come from your own ideas.)

II. PREWRITING

    Look at the piece of art from a distance. Write down all your first impressions of its meaning. How do you feel about it?

III. SELECTING INFORMATION

    A. Move close to it and look carefully at the small details.

    B.   Write down their possible contribution to the overall meaning. (*Note:* As you look at the painting closely, you may decide to change your first impression.)

IV. ORGANIZING THE INFORMATION   Due: _____

    A. Put the details in logical groups.

    B. Decide which groups best support the meaning you see.

    C. Make headings for your groups.

    D. Write a planning outline.

V. WRITING YOUR FIRST DRAFT—
Suggested model: Due: _____

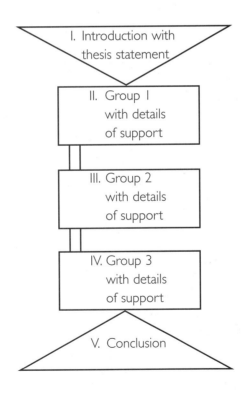

VI. REVISING AND REWRITING   Due: _____

VII. EDITING AND REWRITING   Due: _____

The Evaluation

INTRODUCTION

The most complex model of writing in this course is an evaluation. In an evaluation you:

- Compare and contrast something to an ideal or a standard
- Do an analysis and interpretation to look at parts and determine value to yourself or others
- Defend the values

You have already practiced many of the writing skills you need for an evaluation. In a college setting, you may be asked to evaluate a scientific experiment, graphs and charts, an artistic performance, a solution to a political or social problem, a piece of writing, or a variety of other ideas.

You have probably made this kind of evaluation before. When you exclaimed to friends that a movie was so good that they must see it too, you were using a set of standards in your subconscious mind that helped you decide whether that movie was good or not. Your friends might ask you to tell them why the movie was good. As you answer, they might claim another movie was better, so you tell them the reasons that your movie was the best.

You may have made another evaluation in trying to decide where to go on a date or perhaps even on a vacation. You have a good idea of what a fun date or a great vacation might be. You compare different places to go. You analyze the various options and interpret which would be best. You decide to go one place over another. Sometimes you have to defend your choice to a friend or family member who wants to go somewhere else. Can you think of any other ways you make evaluations?

In an analysis-and-interpretation paper you look at the information and interpret it according to your own ideas. The main difference in an evaluation is that you judge the topic according to a set of standards (points or laws) that are set up before you begin to write. Where can you find this set of standards?

PART 1   *Evaluation: Judging by a Standard*

Standards can come from many sources and have many uses. Some common sources for standards are:

- Experts in the field (scientists, politicians, physicians)

- Person in charge (the boss, the president, the committee chair)

- Popular or majority opinion (polls, votes, buying trends)

Other sources for standards are traditional practices of society or personal decisions about ways to view and live life. These standards can be looked at as:

- Norms of culture, society, or religion

- Parents' expectations

- Personal values

In everyday life, standards are a common way to evaluate your performance or future performance. For example, in this course, standards are used by you and your teacher to evaluate your work and your classmates' work. Score sheets for your papers have been a standard to evaluate those papers and will probably be used to give you a grade for this course. A course grade is a common way of evaluating performance by a standard. Another example is that people sometimes form an opinion about you by looking at your ability to meet cultural norms. When an ESL student said, "I feel anxious because I don't know if I am acting right," she was feeling the pressure of a cultural standard on her behavior.

PART 2   *The Evaluation Process*

If you have read the introduction carefully, you can see that evaluation is a complex process. Here are the parts to preparing an evaluation:

Evaluation Flow Chart

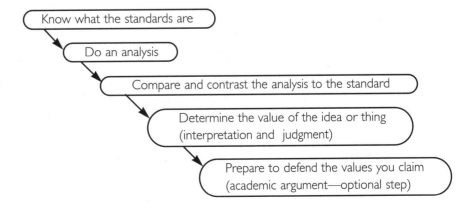

To look at this process, suppose you want to rent an apartment. First, you probably will decide on your needs and how much money you can spend. This is the standard by which you might analyze the details of all the apartments you will look at. As you analyze all the apartments, you make decisions about what you think and feel (interpretation) and decide the value of each apartment (judgment). When you find the apartment that comes the closest to your expectations, you might consider renting that apartment.

Look at how one person went through these steps.

Evaluation of an apartment

Standards (what the person wanted to find)

1. Cost with utilities—no more than $_____ per month
2. Length of lease—no more than one year
3. Distance from work—no more than _____ miles away
4. Number of rooms—bedroom, bath, kitchen
5. Style—modern or new
6. Condition—clean, repaired
7. Parking for car—1 space
8. Pets—no pets, allergic to pet hair

Details observed in an apartment	**Interpretation and judgment of value**
1. $110 more than ideal	1. Ouch! Too much
2. Must sign a year lease	2. Just what I want
3. 2 blocks from work	3. Won't have to drive to work
4. Studio	4. Everything in one room
5. Older style	5. Not my favorite
6. Very clean, new stove	6. Owner cares about this apartment
7. Parking at no extra cost	7. Can save money here
8. No pets allowed	8. No pet hair, no allergy medicine

Here is an evaluation essay using the information from the above chart. Can you see parts of the chart in each paragraph?

Finding an Apartment

You won't believe the trouble I've had looking for a place to live. Good apartments are hard to find. It took me three weeks before I finally found something that fit most of my expectations.

What I wanted was an inexpensive, modern apartment with at least one bedroom, a bathroom, and a kitchen. I wanted the apartment fairly close to my work with no more than a year's lease. I also looked for a place where I could conveniently park my car. Probably just as important as the cost, I needed a clean apartment with no pet hair, so my allergies wouldn't bother me.

The apartment I found is more expensive than I really wanted. However, I will save car money because it is only two blocks from work, and there is no extra charge for parking. Also, since it is very clean and no pets are allowed, I may save money on doctor fees and medicine for my allergies. Even though it is a little old, it is just the size I want. The owner requires a year's lease. My work contract is for a year, so this will be perfect timing.

I don't care for the higher price, but I can save money in other ways, such as in car and medical bills. The good condition of the apartment, the size, and the convenient lease contract make up for it being less modern.

Considering my current needs for an apartment, this apartment is a good choice. It has many of the features I really wanted. Also, by renting this apartment, I will not have to look for another apartment for a year.

PRACTICE 1

Evaluating Your Diet

What did you eat yesterday? Was it an adequate diet? This food guide from the United States Department of Agriculture and the United States Department of Health and Human Services will help you analyze your diet. These charts show the types and the amount of food recommended for a healthful daily diet.

▼ Study the charts and then complete Steps 1 through 4 before writing your evaluation.

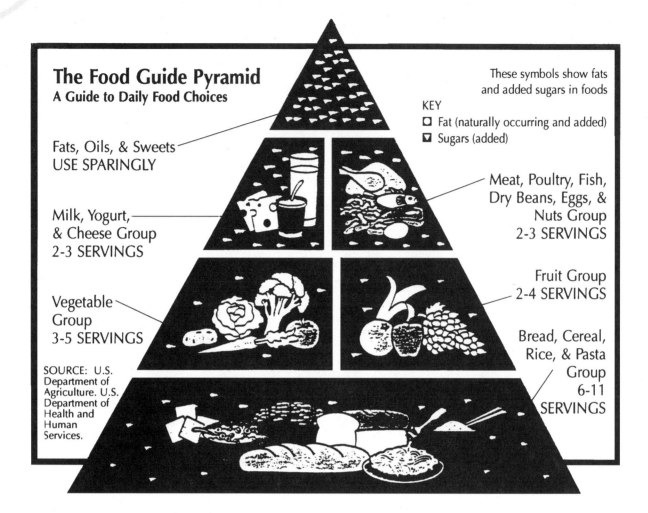

The Food Guide Pyramid
A Guide to Daily Food Choices

These symbols show fats and added sugars in foods

KEY
☐ Fat (naturally occurring and added)
▼ Sugars (added)

Fats, Oils, & Sweets
USE SPARINGLY

Milk, Yogurt, & Cheese Group
2-3 SERVINGS

Meat, Poultry, Fish, Dry Beans, Eggs, & Nuts Group
2-3 SERVINGS

Fruit Group
2-4 SERVINGS

Vegetable Group
3-5 SERVINGS

Bread, Cereal, Rice, & Pasta Group
6-11 SERVINGS

SOURCE: U.S. Department of Agriculture. U.S. Department of Health and Human Services.

How much food is equal to one serving?

Bread, Cereal, Rice, and Pasta	Vegetables	Fruit
1 slice bread	1 cup raw	1 med. piece raw
1/2 cup cooked	1/2 cup cooked	1/2 cup cooked
1 oz. cold cereal	3/4 cup juice	3/4 cup juice

Milk/Yogurt/Cheese	Meat, Poultry, Fish, Dry Beans, Eggs, and Nuts	Fats, Oils Sweets
1 cup milk/yogurt	2–3 oz. cooked meat/poultry/fish	Use sparingly
1.5 oz. cheese	1/2 cup cooked beans	
2 oz. processed cheese	1 egg	
	2 tablespoons peanut butter	

Step 1: Analyze details.

▼ List the foods you actually ate in one day.

Breakfast	Lunch	Supper	Other

Step 2: Combine the food into logical groups.

▼ What did you eat in each food group during one day?

▼ How much of each food did you eat?

Bread	Vegetables	Fruit	Milk	Meat	Fats, Oils, Sweets

Step 3: Compare all the groups with the standard.

▼ Did you eat everything suggested for one day?

Step 4: Make an interpretation and judgment about your diet.

▼ Did you eat enough of each type of food?

▼ Did you eat more of one type of food than suggested?

Step 5: Write an evaluation paragraph in your notebook.

▼ Compare the food you ate to the standard.

In the example below, one student compared his diet to the USDA standard. Then he made a short evaluation. Notice that the student wrote this paragraph by starting with one group and going in order to the others.

Evaluation of My Diet

I usually eat five portions of bread. That includes cereal, rice, or pasta. The minimum according to the Food Guide Pyramid is six servings, so I'm a little behind. I rarely have vegetables in my diet unless they are in soup or another food. I should have three to five servings, so I should eat more vegetables. It is the same with fruit. I should eat two to four servings, but I rarely eat fruit. My three portions of milk are perfect according to the pyramid. I have two portions of meat, poultry, or fish compared to the pyramid that suggests two to three servings, so I'm fine. Finally, I have one serving of sweets, which is OK since the pyramid's recommendation is "little or none." I think I follow the Diet Guide pretty much, but I should eat more vegetables and fruit.

(Javier Cerdio—Mexico)

PART 3 *Evaluation Essay Models*

The evaluation essay includes an evaluation but also describes the standard and discusses the parts of the analysis compared to the standard. Here are two models that show how the parts of an evaluation may be put in an essay. Compare the essay "Finding an Apartment" to these models. Which model does that essay use?

Model 1

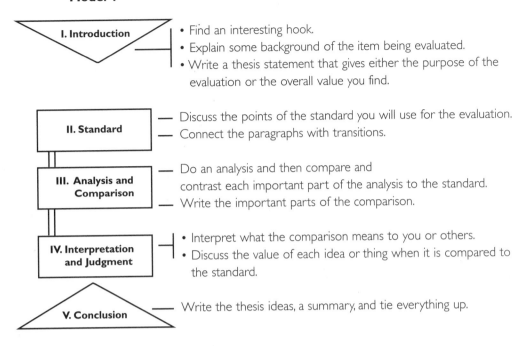

Model 2

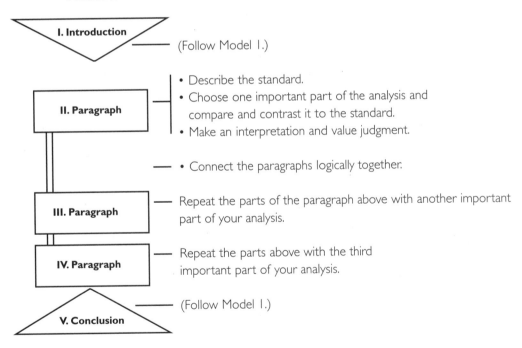

PART 4   *Unit Six Assignment 3: The Evaluation Essay*

To make sure that you understand all of the points you need to cover for an evaluation paper, review the list on page 205.

I. BEGINNING THE ASSIGNMENT

    A. Choose your own topic with the teacher's approval or select one of these topics:

        a part of your school, a community organization

        a book, a program, a solution for a social problem

II. PREWRITING

    A. Brainstorm all you presently know about the topic by asking questions.

    B. Determine the standard you might use to judge the topic.

III. SELECTING INFORMATION

    A. Decide the best place and the best way to find information for your topic.

        1. Look at a school or office or other organization.

        2. Ask questions or observe.

        3. Prepare a personal interview.

        4. Watch a film or television documentary on your subject.

IV. ORGANIZING THE INFORMATION

    A. Do an analysis following each point of your standard.

        1. Compare whether the point is higher, lower, or the same as the standard.

        2. Compare how far the point is from the standard.

    B. Form your interpretation and judgment after comparing the analysis of the details to the standard you set before you began.

    C. Choose those points that will be most interesting for your essay.

    D. Decide what organization model you will use to write the essay.

    E. Make a planning outline.

V. WRITING YOUR FIRST DRAFT

    A. Use one of the evaluation essay organization models.

VI. REVISING AND REWRITING

    A. Add details and examples if necessary to make the meaning clear to the reader.

    B. Reorganize if necessary.

VII. EDITING AND REWRITING

    A. Read your essay aloud.

    B. Correct errors in grammar, spelling, and punctuation.

    C. Use the spell-check feature on your word processor.

Expanding Research Sources

The library is not the only source of information for academic research. In fact, the most recent research is so new that it probably hasn't been published. To get up-to-date information on your topic, you can also use sources such as:

- Personal interviews

- Speeches or lectures

- Television, video, or film

PART 1 *Interviewing*

Guidelines for Interviews

To make an interview successful, here are some guidelines to help you plan your questions, conduct the actual interview, and then evaluate the information after the interview.

Before the interview

1. Be sure to give the reason for the interview and tell how you will use the information.

2. Plan an interview of no more than one hour.

3. Ask the person if he or she is willing to talk to you about a specific topic. Some topics may be sensitive.

4. Request permission to use actual quotations or to make a tape recording of the interview.

5. Prepare questions in writing, but don't be afraid to ask other questions that come up.

During the interview

1. Tell the person the complete purpose of the interview.

2. Write down the date, time, person's name (correctly spelled), position, and his or her relationship to your topic.

3. Begin with the questions you prepared, but ask other questions you may think of during the interview to clarify or add information to the answer.

4. If you find an exciting part of the topic, focus more of your questions on that part.

5. Avoid asking questions in areas the person doesn't want to talk about.

6. Write down important points. The interviewee will not be offended if you take a few minutes to write down his or her words and ideas correctly.

7. Ask the person if there are other important ideas that you forgot or that he or she would like to talk about.

After the interview

1. Be sure to thank the person you interviewed.

2. Ask the person for permission to call later if you need to clarify any point or if you have additional questions.

3. Check the quotations you may want to use. Make sure they are exactly the way the person said them.

4. Revise your notes so that they make sense to you and add information you may have forgotten to write down. Do this as soon as possible after the interview because the longer you wait, the harder it becomes.

5. Make note cards of important parts with key words as soon as possible.

PART 2 *Preparing Interview Questions*

Part of organizing an interview is creating useful interview questions. Questions that are too general or that can be answered with *yes* or *no* are not very useful in an interview.

The best kinds of interview questions help a person talk freely about a topic. They are called open-ended questions. That is, there are no limits to the answer the person might give.

1. Writing open-ended questions

As you write a question, imagine how the person you interview might answer. This will help you find open-ended questions, because they have the most possible answers. Some open-ended questions are not really questions at all, but are statements that lead the interviewee to give you more information.

Meaning	Open-Ended Questions
Explanation	Tell me about _____.
	How did this _____ occur?
	Explain to me about _____.
Personal Opinion	What do you feel about _____?
	What do you think _____?
	Explain what you mean by _____.
	What do you see as the problem?
Suggestions	What do you recommend?
	What can be done?
	What do you suggest?

2. Putting questions in a logical order

If one question or piece of information leads to another in a logical order, the actual interview and taking notes will be easier. If you jump around from one part of the topic to another, it will be hard to take notes because the information comes in small disconnected pieces. Asking questions in an order helps the interviewee feel comfortable and free to share opinions and feelings. Here are three possible ways you might organize your questions.

- General to specific
- Facts to opinions
- Chronological order (What happened first, second, and third?)

These interview questions were prepared for an editor of a magazine. What logical order was used?

Interview Questions

1. What type of person reads your magazine?

2. What do you see as the major concerns of your readers?

3. What concern do you think is the most important?

4. Tell me what this community is doing about this concern.

5. What else do you think should or could be done?

6. Tell me about your experience or someone else's experience who has worked with this problem.

PART 3   *Taking Notes from Interviews*

It may be difficult to hear important information in an interview. However, in speaking, many people use *clue words* that show the organization of their thoughts. These clue words tell you that something important may follow. It's like waving a red flag to tell you to listen carefully to that part of the conversation. This chart shows some common clue words and phrases.

Clue Words and Phrases

Opinion	Facts	Main Ideas
What I suggest is	One fact is	I'll start with
Basically, I think	The fact of the matter is	In the beginning
What I'm thinking is	Statistically	The basic (vital, fundamental,
They are supposed to	Count the cost	root, main) problem is
I believe	The percent of	Today, this is what is happening
It's just that they should	There are ___ of these	My first (second, third) point
What I mean is	Actually, you can see_____	Let's look at the separate parts
You could say	_____is less than (more than)	One fundamental point
I might say	The rate of	Let me give you an example
I agree that ___, but ___	The rise of	Another part of the problem
I'm embarrassed to admit	The forecast is	There are two types of
I'm optimistic that	The minimum (maximum)	This means that
		Before I say anything more
		You remember
		To repeat what I said
		As you can see then
		Maybe I can summarize this way
		To sum it up

PRACTICE 1

Listening for Clue Words

Here is an interview with an editor of a magazine using the questions on page 209.

Follow the directions.

▼ Silently read the interview for understanding.

▼ Now, listen to someone read it. As you listen, put an *X* next to the clue words or phrases.

▼ Read the interview again. Underline the clue words or phrases and count how many you find.

▼ Compare the number of clue words you heard to the number of clue words in the interview. Which clue words are hard for you to hear?

▼ Listen to the interview again. Take notes. Then compare your notes with a classmate's notes. Do you see any differences?

INTERVIEWER: Hello. Are you Catherine Hatch? Your secretary told me you were waiting for me. I'm   *(name)*   from   *(country or area)* .

EDITOR: Yes, come in. I'm glad to meet you. You asked for an interview about the opinions of the people who buy *Today's Action.* Is that right?

INTERVIEWER: Yes, I did.

EDITOR: How can I help you?

INTERVIEWER: Well, maybe before we go any further, I should first make sure that I have your name correctly spelled and your official position. Would you look at what I have written to make sure it's correct?

EDITOR: Right here my name is spelled wrong. *Catherine* starts with a *C* and not a *K.* Everything else is correct.

INTERVIEWER: Thank you. The first question I would like to ask you is, who are your customers? I mean, who reads your magazine?

EDITOR: Most of our readers are adults who live in this city and come from many economic groups. We try to find topics of local interest that most people around here would want to read about. Why do you ask?

INTERVIEWER: I'm writing a paper, and I want to know what the major concern is of most of your readers.

EDITOR: Hmmm. I think the major concern is gang-related crime in our once-peaceful neighborhoods.

INTERVIEWER: Why is that so? Can you give me some background to this problem?

EDITOR: Certainly. From the beginning our city has had poor areas—families who were struggling on very low weekly salaries. But most of the parents taught their children to better themselves with education. The people took pride in their little yards and tried to keep things neat.

INTERVIEWER: What happened to change that?

EDITOR: Gang violence. A small group who had no goals found that gangs brought them the security they didn't have in their homes. As a matter of fact, the growth of gangs was so gradual that we did not see the problem until it got bad. Now drugs play a major role in gang activities.

INTERVIEWER: What is happening now?

EDITOR: It is no longer safe for someone to walk alone on the streets in these areas. As an example, recently, in the middle of the day, a young man was arguing with a female gang member. A strange man who was apparently part of the gang approached the arguing couple and shot the young man in the face. I could tell you many accounts similar to this, but we don't have the time. Basically, the rate of gang-related physical injury and death has doubled within two years.

INTERVIEWER: Is anyone doing anything about this problem?

EDITOR: Yes. As a matter of fact, in one area the citizens decided to take back their neighborhood from gang destruction.

INTERVIEWER: That sounds good. Can I use your exact words, "take back their neighbor-hood from gang destruction"? (*A nod from the editor*) It also sounds dangerous. What are they doing?

EDITOR: In the beginning, one woman tried to organize the people into groups. These groups would watch their streets and report anything that looked wrong. But there was little change. People were too scared. After her son was shot—the one I told you about—this lady got the police to agree to periodic raids or roundups of any strangers in the neighborhood. It was in one of these raids that they caught the man who shot her son. This gave everyone hope that they could make their neighborhood safer. Later, this lady and concerned young people marched through the neighborhood chanting, "Drugs must go! Drugs must go!" Slowly, timid people came out of their apartments to join the march. This created more hope, and many began regularly calling the police whenever they saw a drug-related incident, instead of being fearful. They were organized into block watchers, and some even used binoculars. This was so successful that a group of these people demanded that the police begin raids of the neighboring areas as well.

INTERVIEWER: Let me see then. These are the ways the neighborhood committee uses to solve the problem. I would like to write them down. First, the citizens got together to try to organize themselves, and then they got some more help from the police, then the march helped more people get involved in fighting the crime. Now the police and the people are working together. Is this right?

EDITOR: Yes, that is right. It's starting to be effective in many parts of our state. Let me add that I am optimistic that this cooperation between citizens and police is good. But the fact is, we cannot ever relax our work. Gang violence will continue to be a concern as long as parents don't take the responsibility for teaching their children.

INTERVIEWER: I think so, too. Do you have anything more you would like to share?

EDITOR: Yes. I firmly believe that youth, rich or poor, need to be taught skills and have goals and a belief that they can be what they want to be. I'm embarrassed to admit, however, that I don't know how this can be done quickly enough to help some of our youth.

INTERVIEWER: I have a few more questions, but our time is up, and you have answered them partly already. You have been very helpful. I thank you for your time and your answers to my questions. If I need a little more information, may I call you?

EDITOR: Yes. Certainly. I'm less busy in the afternoons, so that would be the best time to call me. And it has been my pleasure to answer your well-planned questions. I wish you success on your report.

**Now interview someone and make note cards for
your evaluation paper.**

P A R T 4 *Citing Interviews*

When you use material from an interview in your writing, you can quote the person exactly, paraphrase, or summarize. You can tell the reader about the interview by using one of the citation examples below:

1. Explain in your own words that you are using information from a personal interview. Give the name and some data about the person in your paper.

Example:

> Catherine Hatch, editor of *Today's Action* magazine, **revealed in a personal interview on January 10, 1995,** that the major concern of her readers was gang violence. She said that the most effective deterrent to this type of violence is neighborhood organizations that "take back their neighborhood from gang destruction." In this movement, the citizens of an area get together and decide for themselves what can be done to clean up their neighborhood problems with gangs. Volunteers take assignments. Various police departments across the state have been extremely cooperative in working with these neighborhood groups.

2. Put the citation in parentheses immediately after the interview information in this form:

(First initial and Last name, personal communication, date, year)

Example:

> According to the editor, the major concern of *Today's Action* readers is gang violence. The most effective deterrent to this type of violence is neighborhood organizations that "take back their neighborhood from gang destruction." In this movement, the citizens of an area get together and decide for themselves what can be done to clean up their neighborhood problems with gangs. Volunteers take assignments. Various police departments across the state have been extremely cooperative in working with these neighborhood groups. **(C. Hatch, personal communication, January 10, 1995)**

Note: A personal interview is not included in the reference list. This is because the purpose of references is to help the reader find your original source. The reader will probably not be able to find a printed source of the words of the person you interviewed.

PRACTICE 2

*Analyzing an Article
from an Interview*

The example below shows how the information from an interview can be written in a paper.
Follow the directions:

▼ Read the following article, which was written from a telephone interview.

▼ Underline the words that tell the reader that the information is the result of an interview.

▼ Answer this question: Does the writer use Example 1 or Example 2?

Los Angeles Teacher Teaches Math and Hope

The story in the movie *Stand and Deliver,* according to the real-life school-teacher, Jaime Escalante, is 90 percent true. The actor in the film actually wore some of Jaime Escalante's clothing and drove his white VW bug. By challenging his under-achieving basic math class, by forcing them to stretch to his expectations—with extra summer classes, early and late classes, and Saturday classes—Escalante prepared his students for the AP Calculus Exam. And they passed. As the film shows, the number of test-takers has doubled and tripled each year since. This year he has 223 in his AP Calculus class.

In a telephone interview, after his classes at Garfield High School in Los Angeles, Jaime Escalante was willing to explain the lives of the students portrayed in the film. Escalante said that they have—among them—degrees in chemistry, math, anthropology, and engineering, and one has earned a Master's in business. Another is working on a degree in architecture, one has not kept in contact. "And one died in an accident on his way to see the film," Escalante said quietly.

Escalante refuses to take the credit for his students' successes. He considers himself a catalyst and acknowledges the abilities of his students. "Math is not magic. These Cinderellas, once they received their invitation to the ball, worked, earned scholarships, studied, and realized their own possibilities."

Escalante gave up a more profitable career in computers in order to teach. He has since had offers to go elsewhere for more money, but he said in the interview, "I belong here. My place is here."

(Jean Marshall—Adapted and used with permission.)

> **At this point include interview information in your evaluation essay. Be sure to use Citation Examples 1 or 2.**

Applying Writing Skills to Essay Exams

INTRODUCTION

Now that you've developed some skill at writing essays, we will take a look at two of the most important kinds of essays you will be asked to write: the essay exam and a university application essay. Essay exams are particularly challenging, because they usually ask you to go through the writing process in a very short, limited time. By learning to look for key words and by depending on the organization skills you have been working on, you should have some useful strategies for taking this kind of test.

The university application essay is usually not timed, but you must meet a deadline for sending it to the college. In this sort of essay, you are asked to demonstrate your best writing skills while telling about yourself and the things that are important to you. You will be evaluated on your ability to think, plan, organize, and write your ideas logically and clearly. Again, the skills you've been learning will come in handy.

In this unit you will:

▼ Develop strategies for taking essay exams

▼ Evaluate essay-exam questions

▼ Write your own essay-exam questions and answers

You will also learn to:

▼ Write a successful university application essay

Other skills you will practice are:

▼ Using all the essay forms you have used

▼ Using transitions and modals

Essay Exams

INTRODUCTION

The essay examination is more than a test of writing in correct English. It is a test of your ability to:

▼ Think deeply about a topic and determine your own ideas and opinions

▼ Organize your ideas into a logical pattern

▼ Write so that the reader clearly understands your meaning

It requires you to:

▼ Make decisions on what information will best answer the question

▼ Organize the information quickly into a logical writing pattern

▼ Find and choose details that best support your organization

▼ Write the answer rapidly and completely

PART 1 One Student's Experience with Essay Exams

Essay examinations often ask you to write your own opinion, interpretation, or evaluation of the topic. An ESL (English as a Second Language) student named Mai was unsuccessful in her first college essay exams. Read her story. Compare her experience to your own test-taking experiences.

Experiences of an ESL Student at College

Mai was upset. As a first-semester graduate student in public health, she had attended all her classes, taken good notes, done all the reading, and studied hard. After her first exam in nutrition she left the classroom feeling confident about what she had written. She was sure she would get a good grade.

But when the professor returned their exams, Mai's grade was only a C+! What had she done wrong? She searched the paper for a clue. Next to her last answer was this note from her professor: "You know the facts, but I asked you to evaluate the program. Next time let me see some critical thinking along with the statistics."

Mai's experience points out an important characteristic of American higher education. Along with learning facts and acquiring information, in many courses there is an emphasis on evaluating facts and interpreting information. Merely memorizing the content of the textbook or the lectures is not enough. As a college student, you will be expected to draw on the content to formulate inferences and give opinions.

Perhaps, like Mai, you are unclear about the meaning of critical thinking. Briefly, it means "doing your own thinking." You are thinking critically when you see an advertisement on television and say to yourself: "What is the advertiser's hidden message? How are they trying to influence me?" You are thinking critically when you read about a controversial topic in two different sources with opposing views, and say to yourself: "What are the most important arguments for and against? Which statements are facts, and which are opinions, exaggerations, or even misinformation?" Then, using both sources and your own knowledge and experience, you come to your own conclusion.

When Mai came to understand what the professors expected of her, she began to receive better grades on her written assignments and examinations. She learned to watch for words like *criticize, evaluate,* and *justify.* When she saw any of these words in an assignment, she knew that her professor expected a response that went beyond simply restating the information in the textbook.

As time went on, Mai realized that in most of her courses the crucial skill was critical thinking. This meant, for example, that she had to be able to write papers in which she organized and synthesized complex data. She had to be able to read an article and draw her own conclusions based on it. In time, she discovered that doing her own thinking brought her success and personal satisfaction in her academic work.

(Reproduced with permission from Association of American Publishers)

The ultimate test of your writing ability may be a written exam. The TOEFL (Test of English as a Foreign Language) for foreign students has an optional 30-minute essay-exam section called the TWE (Test of Written English), which some universities require. Here are some examples that are similar to essay-exam questions on the TWE.

1. The gasoline engine has had an influence on every society. Discuss the impact of the gasoline engine for better or for worse, and support your opinion with examples.

2. Some people think that a college student should choose a major upon entering college, and others think a student should take time to choose a major. Which position do you take? Explain your position.

3. Applying paint to parts of the body or the face is found in many cultures and has a variety of meanings. Define another important cultural practice and state the impact it has had on your life.

PART 2   *Analyzing the Test Question*

Essay-exam questions are not all written as questions. Some of them are written as commands. The answer will be correct only if you understand the question words or the key words exactly. Notice the key word in this example essay question:

Discuss how advertising influences the buyer's selection of products.

Discuss means "talk about." To answer this question you would talk about various ways that advertising affects a shopper.

Here are some key words that may begin an essay question. After each word is a description of what you would do in your answer.

Support	Give details in examples and facts.
Criticize	Make an analysis and determine the good or bad points.
Outline	Write the main ideas.
Enumerate	Make a list of important parts.
Comment	Say anything you think is important about the topic.

Sometimes one test question will have two or more parts. You must find all the key words of the question in order to determine how many parts should be in the answer. For example, a question might look like this:

Analyze and interpret what happened to the old man in Hemingway's *The Old Man and the Sea.*

This question is asking you to do two things:

1. Analyze tell important parts of what happened to the old man in the story

2. Interpret determine the meaning of these parts in the story

If you only analyzed but did not interpret, you would only have half the answer required in this question.

Test yourself. See if you know the meaning of some common key words used in the essay examination questions.

P R A C T I C E 1

Defining Key Words

▼ Write what you would do if the essay question began with each key word or phrase.

▼ You may use your dictionary, but write what you think you would do in your own words.

1. Define: *tell the meaning of something* _____

2. Report _____

3. Explain _____

4. Summarize _____

5. Describe _____

6. List the steps _____

7. Tell how to_____

8. Show the cause _____

9. Discuss the effect _____

10. Explain or show the cause and effect _____

11. Discuss both sides_____

12. Discuss one side _____

13. Compare *X* to *Y*_____

14. Discuss how *X* is different from *Y* _____

15. Defend _____

16. Argue _____

17. Analyze_____

18. Interpret _____

19. Evaluate _____

P A R T 3 *Test-Taking Strategies*

The essay exam is really a test of many skills. Sometimes when students are under pressure to take an essay exam, they will read the first question and answer that question immediately. Then they will go to the next question. This may seem like a good way to take a test, but it isn't the best way to take an essay exam because you may overlook part of a question or run out of time.

Here are some common mistakes students make in essay exams:

▼ Incomplete answer because there is no time left

▼ Incomplete answer because some parts of the question were missed

▼ Answer doesn't match the question

▼ Too little support for the main ideas

▼ Extra or unnecessary information

▼ Answer is too short

▼ Weak organization of ideas

These mistakes can be avoided if you follow some basic steps. These steps will help you improve your essay-examination scores.

Step 1: Quickly read all the questions.

● Make sure that you understand the test questions. If you don't, ask the teacher before you start.

● Determine how many parts there are in each question. Number the parts.

● Decide which question to begin with or to decide in which order you will answer the questions. Some people like to start with the easiest questions first. Others start with the shortest questions or the hardest questions.

Step 2: Plan your time.

Before you begin writing any answers, plan how you will spend your total test time so you have enough time to:

● Read the test questions carefully.

● Plan how you will divide the total test time.

● Decide which questions you will answer first and how much time you will use.

● Organize and answer the questions, using your time plan.

● Read and make corrections in your answers.

If this circle represented a testing time of 60 minutes, how many minutes would you want to spend on each part of the circle? Write the number of minutes on the sections of the clock drawing.

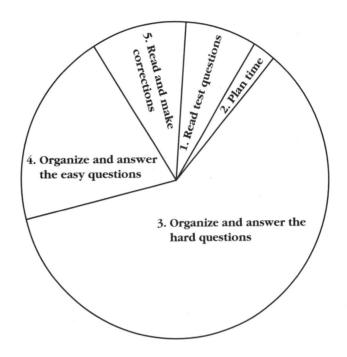

Step 3: Organize each answer.

Don't begin to write immediately. You need to organize your answers. To do this:

- Make some quick notes as you think about the topic, such as outline headings or main ideas with details.

- Ask yourself often, "Will this information answer the question?"

- Write your answer from your organizational plan. Be careful that you have a main idea in each paragraph.

- Write enough to give a complete answer to each key word.

Good organization (topic sentence and supporting details for each point) will increase the correctness of your answer. If the question requires a long answer (several pages) you will probably need an introduction and a conclusion. Short answers usually require well-formed paragraphs. If you are not sure if the answer should be short or long, check with your teacher or test monitor. In any case, choose an organizational model that best fits the question.

Remember to limit your answer to the question that is asked. On the other hand, be careful that you write enough to give a complete answer.

PRACTICE 2

Evaluating Questions and Answers

Read these exam questions and answers taken from real tests. Follow the directions:

▼ Read each question and determine what the key words are asking the student to do.

▼ For part a, explain what kind of answer the key words require.

▼ For part b, explain how the student did not follow the key words in the answer.

Example:

Test Question: Describe your college writing class.

Student Answer: I like it.

a. The test question requires the student to write a paragraph about the class with some details about the class.

b. The student answer was a personal opinion instead of a description with details. It is too short for an essay examination.

Test: Gomera Island and Whistle-Language

In the following test, the students incorrectly answered essay-exam questions about an article on the topic of a language without words. (The people on Gomera can communicate meaning by whistling in particular ways.)

1. **Test Question:** How do people learn whistle-language?
    Student Answer: Because it is a hundred years old.

    a. _____

    b. _____

2. **Test Question:** Explain why whistle-language got started and summarize the uses of the whistle-language.
    Student Answer: The whistle-language is used in many ways. It is used to communicate to people across the valleys. It is used to relay a message into the city when someone is sick or injured or when a boy tending the cattle needs help. It is also used on the waterfront.

    a. _____

    b. _____

3. **Test Question:** Describe the people who have lived on Gomera Island and tell about the legend of the origin of whistle-language.
    Student Answer: The Norman seamen cut the tongues of the people. For this reason they had to whistle instead of talk.

    a. _____

    b. _____

4. **Test Question:** Outline the important parts of this article.
   Student Answer: An outline is made with Roman numerals. It has headings and subheadings of main ideas. It has five parts. The first is the introduction, then three parts of the body, and then the conclusion. The outline is important to have before writing a paper.

   a. _____

   b. _____

PRACTICE 3

Answering Essay Questions

Now it is your turn to use all you have learned to write answers to essay questions on the topic of why children lie (fib).

▼ Read these two articles.

▼ Make marginal notes.

▼ Answer the essay questions following the articles on a separate piece of paper.

Article 1

Why Kids Fib

You've just noticed that a cupcake is missing from the dozen you've set out for your child's preschool party. The cat doesn't look guilty, but your three-year-old, hiding under the kitchen counter licking her fingers, sure does. When you confront her, she proclaims innocence: "No, Mommy, I didn't take it."

Whether the offense is a stolen sweet or crayon marks on the wall, most parents are distressed when they catch their children in a lie. But nearly all kids—even very young ones—fib, says Michael Lewis, Ph.D., a professor of pediatrics and psychiatry at the Robert Wood Johnson Medical College in New Brunswick, New Jersey. In one study, he secretly videotaped children ages two and a half through seven after a researcher set an elaborate toy behind them and instructed the kids not to "peek." Not only did 70 percent of the youngsters spin around to investigate the toy after the researcher left the room, but later, when asked if they'd looked, a full 85 percent of the peekers said no. (Among the oldest children in the study, nearly 100 percent fibbed about their actions.)

What should parents do when they know their kids aren't telling the truth? First, resist the impulse to yell, "You lied to me!" advises Dr. Lewis. Children fib for an obvious reason—to avoid punishment—so focus on the misdeed, rather than the particular cover-up. Explain why it's wrong to take another child's doll or to decorate the couch with tyrannosaurus stickers, then work out appropriate "restitution." Having your child return the doll with an apology or help you remove the stickers (or a brief time-out in his room as punishment) will reinforce your lesson.

But if your child is a chronic liar, says developmental psychologist Carolyn Saarni, Ph.D., of Sonoma State University in Rohnert Park, California, consider whether you're spending enough time with him. He may be acting naughty to get your attention and then lying to avoid the consequences. Only by asking yourself some probing questions—and answering them honestly—can you help a deceiving child become a truth teller too.

(Kathryn E. Livingston, Michael Lewis, and Carolyn Saarni—
Used with permission.)

Article 2

From Two to Twelve: How Lies Grow Up

Your reading glasses are missing from your nightstand, and when you find them—stashed behind the sofa cushions—they're broken. You've repeatedly warned your child about touching your things, know that he's guilty, and confront him. Here, says Carolyn Saarni, Ph.D., is what he's likely to answer.

Ages 2 to 4: *"No, Mommy, I didn't break your glasses!"* At this age, children understand they have broken a rule and begin to be able to deny it. They are also capable of thinking *"If I say yes, I may get in trouble."*

Ages 5 to 7: *"Not me. But Skippy was jumping on the couch before."* School-age children will not only deny they are the agents, but can generate alternative causes, shifting the blame.

Ages 8 to 10: *"I don't know how they got broken, Mom, but I sure hope you can get them fixed. Maybe the store can glue them."* At this age, children realize that if you discover they are lying, you may be even angrier. So they may offer a word of comfort or a solution.

Ages 10 to 12: *"No, Mom. It's not my job to keep track of your glasses, but I did notice that you left them on the couch where they could get broken really easily."* By preadolescence, children can set up smokescreens to try to convince you they are not responsible. They are also able to rationalize, convincing themselves they had no role in the mishap.

Most kids don't realize that even with their glasses off, parents can usually see the truth!

(Kathryn E. Livingston and Carolyn Saarni—Used with permission.)

Essay Questions

1. Explain the study of Dr. Lewis in your own words and tell why you think more older children in his study told lies.

2. Tell why children "fib," give an example from your life or the life of someone you know, and explain if lying is ever justified.

3. What should you do if your own child fibs?

P A R T 4 *Preparing for Writing Your Own Essay Exam*

Creating your own essay-exam questions will help you understand the process your instructors use in writing a test. In this section, you will create questions that could be used on a final exam for this course.

How are test questions designed? How will you know what kind of questions to prepare? Here are some important standards for writing test questions. They should:

- ask about the important points of the course.

- be easy to understand and not too complex.

- state clearly the type of information expected in the answer.

P R A C T I C E 4

Evaluating Essay-Exam Questions by the Standards

▼ Read the test questions and fill in the chart

Test Question	What does the question ask you to do?	Is there a problem with the question? If so, what is it?
1. What is research?		
2. Give four characteristics of a good research question and explain each with details.		
3. Why is there a need for more than one kind of research approach?		
4. Discuss the advantages and disadvantages of library research.		
5. What are the steps in library research? Put them in chronological order.		

PART 5   *Unit Seven Assignment: The Essay Exam*

For this assignment you will need to write:

- five test questions, each of which requires a different type of answer
- at least one question that requires several parts in the answer
- the correct answers to your questions

Follow the steps for writing an essay exam as you do this assignment.

Step 1: Select information.

Before you begin, think of some of the most important things you have learned. Make some notes of the major ideas. Your questions will come from your ideas.

Step 2: Prepare the questions.

Now you are ready to begin writing the questions. As you prepare them, ask yourself:

- Considering the answer that I want, what is the best way to write the question?
- How complex should the question be?

For instance, you may want an answer that requires an explanation and some examples. How can you best write the essay question, and how will the students clearly know that you expect two parts in their answer? You might write:

> What are the differences between a pro-con issue and an academic-argument issue and what is an example of each type?

Is this clearer?

> Explain the differences between a pro-con issue and an academic-argument issue. Give an example of each.

Step 3: Prepare the answers.

When you write an essay-exam question for this course, also write a possible answer. By doing this, you are creating the **answer key,** which is the *standard* by which the students' answers will be scored. Here is an example of how your test questions and answer key should look.

Exam Question:

What is research?

Answer Key

Research is the process of finding specific information that explains, supports, and therefore answers a research question. There are basically two kinds of research: original research and library research. Original research is figuring out the answers by yourself, using a method or combination of methods, such as observation, experiments, interviews, and surveys, and then writing down the entire process and the conclusions. Library research is looking for the answer (or support for a possible answer) to a research question in the library by reading what others have done or reported. All research needs to have proper citations and references for the sources.

When you finish, you should have five exam questions and five answer keys.

Step 4: Give your test.

Write your essay questions on a separate piece of paper and give your test to a classmate to answer.

Step 5: Evaluate your classmate's answers.

Compare the classmate's answers to your answer key. Ask yourself:

- Was the answer what you expected?
- Did the answer leave out necessary information?
- Did the answer give unnecessary information?

Give your classmate a score for each answer. Your total test will be worth 50 points. You must decide how many points each answer should receive.

Step 6: Revise your test and answer key.

Improve your test by discussing your examination questions with a classmate and evaluating which ones are best and why. There may be problems in the way you formed the question, or you may need better instructions or key words. Maybe the essay question was too easy or too hard. Maybe you have forgotten important parts of the answer in your answer key.

> **Turn in your improved questions and answers to your instructor for possible use in your final examination.**

The University Application Essay

INTRODUCTION

The application essay required by a college or university when you apply to enter is very much like an essay examination. You will be evaluated on many skills such as your ability to think, plan, organize, and write your ideas logically and clearly in English.

There are two major differences between an application essay and an essay examination. One difference is that the application essay has no time limit. You can use all the time you have available until the date you must send it to the university. It is like a *take-home test* in which you can use all your resources to write your answer at home. Another difference is that the subject is personal. The topic is you and your possible future relationship with that university.

Since every university or college application is a little different, this chapter is designed to give you some basic information.

PART 1 *The Application Essay Question*

The application essay question is only one part of the entire application. Depending on the question, your answer may be a long essay from one to five pages, a letter, or individual paragraphs.

The audience will most likely be adult employees of the university or college. The audience can be one person, a group of writing experts, or an application committee or board.

There are several purposes for an application essay question:

- to evaluate your ability to write in English
- to determine your character, individuality, and creativity
- to see if your goals are compatible with the university's goals
- to judge your writing maturity

The content of essay questions asked by leading universities is often similar because they reflect the general purposes above. Here are some questions they might ask on the application:

Why did you choose to apply to this university or college?

What are your future goals and how do they meet goals of the university?

What makes you an interesting or unique person?

What difficulties in life have you faced that have improved your character?

What activities have you been involved in outside of schoolwork that have broadened you as a person?

What can you contribute to make this university a better place?

All essay questions should be written only by you. Some universities are very strict and do not want you to get any help at all with the writing process. In this case, the essay is a test in which you write just one draft on the application itself. Other universities want you to give them your final draft after you have gone through the writing process. Even though you may write many drafts and consult with others for direction, revision, and editing, the final result must represent your own writing abilities.

P A R T 2 *Proving Your Writing Ability*

One purpose for the essay is to evaluate your ability to write in English. This ability includes knowing how to use the skills and strategies for taking essay exams that you have studied. It also means knowing how to follow the writing process taught through each unit of this course.

Most schools read your essay and compare it to the other application essays they receive at the same time. When thousands of essays come into a large school, it is easy to compare writing abilities and to see common mistakes. Here is a list of problems that are often seen on application essays and a list of what these mistakes often mean to the people who read them.

Problem	Possible Meaning
Student doesn't follow the intructions.	Student may not understand enough English to be admitted.
Student joins sentences together in an unorganized way.	Student doesn't understand English organizational patterns.
Answer is either too long or too short.	Too short: the student is lazy or uninterested.
	Too long: the student is trying too hard to impress people or hasn't learned to write concisely.
Student gets off the subject.	Student can't write in expository English organizational patterns.
Student's handwriting is illegible and the paper is messy.	Student can't type, doesn't know what a paper should look like, or doesn't care.
Student writes without planning.	Student is not serious about the application.
Student writes in a conversational style including slang words.	Student doesn't know the formal vocabulary and style used in academic writing.

If you want to make a positive impression with your application essay, avoid these problems.

PART 3 *Analyzing your Character, Individuality, and Creativity*

Depending on the application essay question, you probably will be asked to write about those areas in your life that show your unique positive characteristics in comparison to the other students who will most likely apply to the same university.

For many students, it is hard to identify their positive attributes and talents, and it is difficult for them to write about themselves. The example below shows how one student successfully found positive characteristics in her life. Can you identify all the positive parts of her life that she chose to write about?

Example

> In Japan I worked at a hospital and studied nursing. I went on the train early in the morning and returned late at night every day. Sometimes I was exhausted. Sometimes I wanted to quit. But I didn't. Even though I am an older student, I think I can work hard and not quit when I come to the United States.
>
> *(Yuko Matsuoka—Japan. Adapted and used with permission.)*

This student is not alone. Many international students have trouble identifying their unique personal attributes, abilities, and talents, and have trouble deciding what would impress a college application judge.

Here is an exercise to help you prepare for this task. Use it to help you think deeply about the positive things in your life that make you a unique person.

PRACTICE 1

Making a Personal Analysis

▼ Analyze your past, including your experiences in and out of school. Ask the analysis and interpretation questions (pp. 205–206).

▼ Fill in the chart with a list of information.

▼ Choose important details and organize them.

▼ Write a short paragraph.

Nationality, Language	Travel	Difficult Experiences	Characteristics
Service to Others	Talents	Awards, Honors	Clubs
Successful Experiences	Jobs	Sports	Hobbies

Add any other ideas you may have:

PART 4 *Comparing Your Goals to the University Goals*

Often an application essay question will ask you to tell about your professional goals and to explain why you think that university is the right place for you to study. This is really a comparison-and-contrast question. Before you can begin writing, you must identify your own goals. Then you must find information about the university in order to identify the overall university goals and the more specific goals of the department of your major. You may find this information by studying the catalog, talking to a graduate or a current student, and talking with an advisor for that university. After you have gathered this information, you can prepare to write by doing a comparison and contrast with a Venn diagram or an idea chart.

PRACTICE 2

Comparing and Contrasting Goals

▼ Choose a university you are interested in attending.

▼ Study the overall goals of that university and the specific goals of a department you are interested in.

▼ Draw a diagram like this one, and fill it in with your goals and the university's goals. Write the goals you have in common in the center circle.

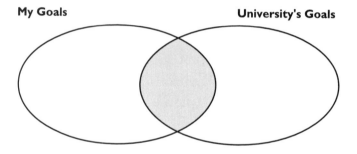

Once you have identified what you will compare and contrast, you are prepared to discuss how your goals are similar. The more similar goals you have, the more compatible you are with that university.

PART 5 *Showing Maturity in Your Writing*

To prove your maturity in your application essay, you must show some characteristics of a mature writer. How will the application committee know that your writing is mature?

Some characteristics that the essay judges will be looking for are your ability to think for yourself and your ability to follow instructions.

1. Thinking for yourself

This means that you can express your own ideas and opinions. It means that you have thought about a subject and have come to some conclusions of your own. At the beginning of this unit you read an article about an ESL student named Mai who was having problems taking an essay exam. Here is an important part of that article:

> Perhaps, like Mai, . . . using both sources and your own knowledge and experience, you come to your own conclusions. . . . She discovered that doing her own thinking brought her success and personal satisfaction in her academic work.
>
> *(Association of American Publishers)*

Writing your own thoughts as an independent person is an important part of the application essay.

2. Following instructions

A mature person usually can follow instructions, so be sure you are exact in doing all the application essay question requires. If the essay question asks you to write a paragraph, don't write an essay. If the question asks you to write an essay, don't write a paragraph. Also, be sure to stay on the topic of the question.

Some of the instructions may be very complex. Just like an essay examination, it is not unusual to find that the question has more than one part. Here is a two-part question that is similar to the questions used by a leading university. Examine this student's answer. Did the student follow the instructions?

Example Question

> Write a paragraph about one area in which you are outstanding and explain why this would make you an asset to this institution.

Example Answer

> The most important personal attribute I can contribute to your university is the fact that I understand another culture and speak Spanish quite well. As a child I lived and went to school in Guatemala, Chile, and Costa Rica for eight years. I became sensitive to the problems of international students and I learned about other ways to view life. I hope my experiences will help the students I associate with.
>
> *(R. E. M. Spencer—United States. Adapted and used with permission.)*

Sometimes deciding what the instructions mean is a difficult task. You can use your skills for analyzing test questions to help you.

P R A C T I C E 3

Following Instructions

Analyze this application essay question carefully to determine the exact instructions.

Answer the questions below.

> Write a one- to three-page statement of your future academic goals including why you chose those goals and why you want to study at this university. Describe your education and your work experience. Additionally, explain what you did in any period of time when you were not in school or working. Include personal data (with dates) of awards, community service, talents, leadership, and significant experiences. Add any other information that would support your application.

▼ How long is the answer?

_____

▼ What parts are asked for?

_____

▼ What could you do to prepare to write?

_____

▼ What writing model could you use?

_____

P A R T 6 *Meeting the Challenge*

Writing the answer to an application essay question is a complex task. It requires that you use all the abilities you have developed in this course to prove that you can write well in English. It examines your knowledge of the goals of the university or college of your choice and asks you to define your own goals. It is also a test to see if you have character, individuality, creativity, and writing maturity.

The application essay is an important test. It may be the deciding factor as to whether you will be admitted to the university or college of your choice.

P R A C T I C E 4

Accepting the Challenge

▼ Write answers to your own university or college application essay questions. You may also want to answer the application question in Practice 3 above.

Appendix

References in APA Style

1. Encyclopedia article

(*Note:* Encyclopedias are seldom used as a reference in a college research paper.)

Form: Author's last name, Initials. (year). Title of article. In Name of first editor et al. (Eds.), <u>Name of Encyclopedia</u> (Vol. #, page number/s). Location: Name of publisher.

Example: Pixton, E. A. (1980). Cotton production. In J. Smith et al. (Eds.), <u>Encyclopedia of Economy</u> (Vol. 3, pp. 952–953). London: Blackwell & Sons, Ltd.

2. Encyclopedia article, no author

Form: Title of article. (year). In Name of first editor et al. (Eds.), <u>Name of Encyclopedia</u> (Vol. #, page number/s). Location: Name of publisher.

Example: Cotton. (1985). In N. Yeld et al. (Eds.), <u>William's Encyclopedia</u> (Vol. 4, p. 850). New York: Littleton Press.

3. Professional journal article

Form: Author's last name, Initials. (year). Title of article. <u>Name of Journal</u>, Vol. #, page numbers.

Example: Paivio, A. (1975). Perceptual comparisons through the mind's eye. <u>Memory & Cognition</u>, 3, 635–647.

4. Magazine article

Form: Author's last name, Initials. (year, month day). Title of article. <u>Name of Magazine</u>, page numbers.

Example: Johnson, J. (1991, June 13). Is America becoming dishonest? <u>Men and Women Today</u>, pp. 70–76.

5. Newspaper article

Form: Author's last name, Initials. (year, month day). Title of article. <u>Name of newspaper</u>, page number.

Example: O'Leary, K. (1992, February 14). Ethical decisions a part of everyday existence, speaker tells students. <u>The Daily Universe</u>, p. 4.

6. Newspaper article, no author

Form: Title of article. (year, month day). Name of newspaper, page number.

Example: Bush outlines aid to former republics. (1992, April 2). <u>Langley Gazette</u>, p. B1.

7. Book with one author

Form: Author's last name, Initials. (year). <u>Title of book</u>. Location: Publisher.

Example: Burley, D. (1994). <u>Holidays in France</u>. Paris: Furtado Books, Inc.

8. Book without author, with editors

Form: Names of editors. (Eds.). (year). <u>Title of book</u>. Location: Publisher.

Example: Newton, F., & Francum, P. (Eds.). (1989). <u>Africa, a land of plenty</u>. New York: York Associates.

9. Book without author or editor

Form: <u>Title of book</u>. (year). Location: Publisher.

Example: <u>Helps for freshmen</u>. (1992). Salt Lake City, UT: University Press.

10. Book with two to four authors

Form: Names of authors. (year). <u>Title of book</u>. Location: Publisher.

Example: Gilly, M., Johnson, D., O'Dell, E., & Graham, R. (1986). <u>American customs reviewed</u>. Chicago: Molland Publishers.

11. Lectures or speeches published

Form: Last name, First Initials. (Date). Title. Publication information if available.

Example: Christensen, A. E. (1994, June 8). Let them eat cake. Dayton, OH: Institute for Nutrition, Lecture 27.

12. Paper (unpublished, but read at a meeting)

Form: Last name, Initials. (Year). <u>Title of paper presentation</u>. Place presented.

Example: Spencer, C. M. (1990, March). <u>Core cultural values of Spanish-speaking ESL students</u>. Paper presented at the Intermountain TESOL meeting, Ogden, UT.

13. Television programs, news broadcasts, documentaries

Form: Producer's last name, Initials. (Individual or network that produced the program). (Year, month day.) Title of specific program. Name of general program. [Type of source]. Head office of the distributor if possible: Name of the distributor.

Example: Bryner, K. (ZUCR).(1993, February 18). Development of children from 8 to 12 months. Day to Day at Home. [Television program]. San José, Costa Rica: ZUCR Network.

14. Video, film

Form: Name, Initials. (Function of person making the production). (year). Title of work. [Type of source]. place: Name of distributor.

Example: Spencer, C. M. (Producer), & Arbon, B. J. (Director). (1994). How to ruin a promising vacation. (Video). Provo, UT: Homeworks.

Transitions

▼ **Conclusion:** Thus,   In short,   In conclusion,

                 Therefore,   In summary,   To conclude,

                                To summarize,

Examples:

- To introduce a quick summary of the main points:

  (In short, In summary, To summarize,) there are three main ways that people should prepare themselves for employment: Study the job market to see what . . .

- Often used in the last sentence of a conclusion:

  (Thus, Therefore,) one must have the proper training and necessary skills in order to find good employment.

- May be used in both of the above ways.

  To conclude, In conclusion,

▼ **Additional Information:**   and   also   too

                                       Another   Furthermore,   Moreover,

                                       In addition,

Examples:

The country was in confusion, **and** the President couldn't do anything about it.

The President decided to call a special session of Congress. He **also** wanted to call together some important political leaders.

He called the governors of the states, **too.**

Another group he called was the Cabinet.

The President decided to call a special session of Congress. **Furthermore, (Moreover, In addition,)** he was considering bringing the governors together.

▼ **Clarification:** In fact,   As a matter of fact,   That is,   In other words

Examples:

There are some people who like Gloria Estefan. **In fact,** they adore her!

As a matter of fact, there are people who worship the ground she walks on.

That is, (In other words,) they follow after her, watch or keep track of her every move, buy every recording she makes, and organize "Gloria Estefan" fan clubs.

▼ **Examples:**   For example,   For instance,   To illustrate,   such as

Examples:

Firefighters must receive training to be effective. **For example, (For instance,)** they must learn how to protect themselves from various kinds of fires and how to rescue people from all sizes of buildings.

To illustrate their ability, the firefighters demonstrated rescuing people from high-rise buildings on the corner of Main and Center Streets yesterday at noon.

They did activities **such as** climbing tall ladders to open windows on the seventh floor, carrying stuffed figures down the ladders over their shoulders, and dropping the figures into safety nets.

▼ **Cause:** Because . . . , because   Since . . . , since   For this reason

Examples:

Because (Since) he got to class late, he started the final exam 30 minutes after the rest of the students.

He started the final exam 30 minutes after the rest of the students **because (since)** he got to class late.

He got to class late. **For this reason,** he started the final exam 30 minutes after the rest of the students.

▼ **Effect:** Consequently, As a consequence, As a result, ; therefore,

Examples:

Consequently, (As a consequence, As a result, In effect,) his grade was lower than he hoped.

He started the final exam late; **therefore,** his grade was lower than he hoped.

▼ **Meaningful order**

First,	Second	After	Last
First of all,			
Before	Now	After that,	
One way	Next		Finally
Another way	More important		Most important

Examples:

Scientists try to explain why dinosaurs became extinct. **First, (First of all,)** they think the world became colder. **Second, (Next,)** they think the colder temperature destroyed many plants that dinosaurs ate. **Finally, (Last,)** they think dinosaurs didn't adapt to these new conditions.

Before scientists realized the big bones of dinosaurs were from an extinct group of animals, they thought they were mammoth bones. **After** they collected all the bones they could find, they put them together.

Now when scientists find dinosaur bones, they put them in plaster. **Later** they carefully take off the plaster and reconstruct the skeletons.

One way to take off the plaster is with small chisels. **Another way** is with soft brushes.

It is important to study fossil bones where they are found. **More important** is to study the position they are in and the surroundings of the site. **Most important** is to carefully preserve the bones for posterity.

Comparison of similarities

▼ **Between sentences or paragraphs**

Similarly,   Likewise,   Also,

Examples:

Both of the men are tall, dark, and handsome. **Similarly, (Likewise, Also,)** both of their wives are tall, dark, and beautiful.

▼ **Between words and phrases within the paragraph**

(just) like	both . . . and	alike	similar (to)
the same (as)	not only . . . but also	compared to	so . . . that

Examples:

Both of the men looked **just like** brothers. They **both** had blond, wavy hair **and** piercing blue eyes. They looked **so** much alike **that** from a distance we could not tell them apart. Actually they were more **similar** than some twins I once knew. They even acted **similar to** each other. **Not only** did they act and look alike, **but** they **also** had same-sounding voices. It was very confusing!

Contrast (differences)

▼ **Between sentences or paragraphs**

On the other hand,   In contrast,   However,

Examples:

On the other hand, (However,) these two men are different in some aspects. John has a quiet nature and is sensitive. **In contrast,** Sam is loud and is concerned mostly about himself.

▼ **Between words and phrases within the paragraph**

Although	While	But	Differ from
Though	Whereas	More than	Different from
Even though	Yet	-er than	Unlike

Examples:

Some of their differences are not very obvious. **Although (Though)** they both have blue eyes, Sam's eyes are dark blue and John's are powder blue. **Even though (While)** they are both tall, John is slimm**er than** Sam, who has a round**er** waist. Also, John's nose is **different from** Sam's because Sam's nose is long**er** and wid**er**. **Yet,** the biggest differences are in their personalities. John's nature is most **unlike** Sam's because he is soft-spoken and gentle, **whereas** Sam is loud and sure of himself. Also, the way John handles problems differs from Sam's. John is methodical and careful, **but (while)** Sam is impulsive in all his decisions.

▼ **Reason**

for	because	since	as
because of	due to	so that	in order to

Examples:

Since (Because) freedom of speech is a part of the constitution of the United States, all immigrants should be allowed to speak their native language whenever and wherever they choose. **Due to (Because of)** the fact that it is hard to find work if you can't understand English, people will discover on their own that **in order to** be paid well, they will have to learn English. For the U.S. government to make everyone learn English is against freedom of speech.

▼ **Result**

as a result	as a consequence	therefore	so
the reason for	consequently	because	thus
For these reasons	Because of these reasons		

Examples:

As a result (As a consequence) of the U.S. government possibly making English official, government papers will not be printed in any other language. **Therefore, (Thus, So, Consequently,)** this will save the taxpayers money.

▼ **Exception or alternative**

although	either	except	if	in spite of
when	even though	instead of	otherwise	yet
rather	still	unless	while	

Examples:

Instead of requiring all people who live in the U.S. to know English, perhaps it should only be required if the person wishes to become a citizen. If this were the case, maybe the argument would stop.

In spite of some efforts to stop the English-only move, lawmakers are becoming more and more in favor of the idea. **Unless** freedom-loving groups unite to educate the public, the freedom to use one's native language in every situation will be lost.

Freedom-loving groups must work together. **Otherwise,** English will become the official language sooner than they think.

While it is important to save money, it is more important to save our freedom of speech.

▼ **Generalization**

    as a general rule   in general   generally

Examples:

As a general rule, (In general, Generally,) the majority of the people who live in the U.S. speak English at home, at work, and at school and play.

▼ **Certainty**

obviously	naturally	certainly	unquestionably
admittedly	of course	even now	surely

Examples:

Obviously, (Naturally, Certainly, Unquestionably, Admittedly, Surely, Of course,) a person from another country who lives and works in the U.S. will want to learn the English language. **Even now,** most immigrants try to learn English as fast as possible.

Index